I Didn't Know You Could Make Birthday Cake from Scratch

Parenting Blunders from Cradle to Empty Nest

by
Dorothy Rosby

Cover design by Sage Stossel. Book design by HumorOutcasts Press.

Published 2016 by HumorOutcasts Press
Printed in the United States of America

ISBN: 0-692-67213-3
EAN-13: 978-069267213-6

For Isaac

I Didn't Know You Could Make Birthday Cake from Scratch 1
A Brief Explanation about How This Book Works (Or Doesn't): 4

I. Postpartum Preoccupation.. 5
Picking the Bathroom Lock and Other Lessons of Motherhood 6
J.K. Rowling, Julia Roberts and Me.. 8
Postpartum Preoccupation..10
Let Them Eat Cake—or Crayons 13
Are You Going to Eat That?...15
Into the Mouths of Babes 18
You Can Lead a Child to Potty but You Can't Make Him Go.....................20
Finding Peace in Play Land..22
Decisions about Sick Kids Make Parents Ill 24
Dead People at the Daycare...27
Will Sweetiekins Give the Steak Knifey Back to Daddy? 29

II. Take It Outside! You're Driving Me Nuts 32
Put the Gun Down and Come Eat Your Breakfast 33
Here Comes Santa Claus (Oh, Goodie)..36
Changing Socks Barbie 38
Why It's Impossible to Clean a Child's Bedroom......................................41
Quality of the Costume Won't Affect the Quantity of the Take 44
Pink is Camouflage if You're Hiding in a Flowerbed 46
Fish Hooks Boy...48
The Ones That Didn't Get Away...50
Pets Teach Responsibility—to Parents...52
Three Goldfish, Two Hamsters and a Canary 54
Break Bread over Their Heads 60
Winning the Birthday Party Competition 63
If This Is so Fun, Why Is Everyone Screaming? 68

III. Keeping Your Kids Enthused about School and
You Enthused about Them 71
Walking Backwards to Kindergarten 72
Keep Your Kids Enthused about School and You Enthused about Your Kids 74
Attack of the Backpack 78
How Long Will it Take Dorothy to Do 22 Math Problems? 81
Snowstorms Not What They Used to Be..83
Wiggling Your Way to Spiritual Growth 85
Give Children Chores So You Don't Have to Do Them 87
Fine Line between a Home-Cooked Meal and a Kitchen Fire 90
Give Kids an Allowance So You Can Borrow from Them Later...................92
Daycare is For Babies, and You Can't Make Me Go Anymore 95

IV. Over-Scheduled Child Ever-Tired Mom **98**
You're Going to Be in Everything and You're Going to Like It 99
The Beginnings of Baseball Players and Unattractive Parents 102
Benched Again.. 105
The Elephant in the Living Room... 107
Get Out Your Checkbook 109
Stay Calm and Don't Die: Lessons from the Car Pool 111
The Helicopter Parent's Guide to Camp 113

V. Family Life is Like a Zoo with the Lions Loose..**115**
Wise Mother Heads off Stressors... 116
Princess Charlotte Elizabeth Diana of Cambridge,
    Don't Make Me Tell You Again... 119
The Ill-Mannered, Obnoxious Babysitter 121
Character Building in the Bathroom 123
Do No Harm. Or, at Least, Don't Do Much Harm 125
Hotdish a la King Again?... 128
You Do Not Need a Plate for Pie 131
Another Garage Sale Foiled 133

VI. Don't Bother Me! I'm Busy Writing a Book about Good Parenting **135**
Celebrating the Finder in Chief... 136
Get Yourself a Man Purse 138
Nonsense and Momsense 140
Life in the Chicken Coop 142
I Should Be Better at This.. 144

VII. No More Pencils, No More Books, No More Teenager's Dirty Looks.....**147**
Don't Bite the Hand That Pays for Your Braces.. 148
Worry Works 150
Life, Liberty and the Pursuit of a New Ford Mustang 152
You're All Minnows Now 154
Job Hunting with Sweet Cheeks 157
An Empty Nest Full of Sour Milk... 160

Acknowledgements

Thank you to my wonderful son Isaac who grew up before the eyes of my column readers and took it all in stride. Thank you also to Wayne, my partner in parenting and in life, who just happens to be a retired elementary school principal. It's a profession that comes with a useful skill set when your child has five friends over for a sleepover. I'd also like to acknowledge my parents, Slim and Elsie. I really should be better at parenting; I had amazing role models.

Finally, thank you to my editor and friend Karen Hall, to my incredible cover designer Sage Stossel, and to the gang at HumorOutcasts Press.

I Didn't Know You Could Make Birthday Cake from Scratch
Parenting Blunders from Cradle to Empty Nest

If you're an Imperfect Parent—as I am—you've had two conflicting thoughts running through your head since the earliest stages of your children's lives:

      1) No one can care for my children better than I can, and

      2) I have no idea what I'm doing.

The latter is reinforced daily by other parents telling amazing stories of their "wonder children," some of which may even be true. The former is not reinforced at all.

As an Imperfect Parent you certainly don't need anyone else casting doubt about your parenting skills; that's your children's job. But the damage is soon done. You begin to compare yourself to other parents and your children to their children. You begin to question your every parenting decision. You become jealous, anxious and mean. In short, you become the kind of person you never want your children to be...or see.

An acquaintance tells you her first grader jumps out of bed, gets dressed, makes her bed and runs into the kitchen to get her own breakfast, all without being told. You ask sarcastically why her 18-year-old is still in first grade—and why she's running in the house. Secretly you wish your 15-year-old would do so well.

Your friend tells you her daughter eats a variety of foods including fruits, vegetables, whole grains and dairy. You agree that, yes, your son also eats a wide variety of foods: seven different kinds of cereal and any type of doughnut.

Every day your neighbor's son dresses nicely in khaki pants and a button down shirt. Meanwhile, your daughter had to ransack the dirty clothes this morning to find something to wear. The item with the least visible grime was a pair of leggings with a hole in one knee.

Another neighbor tells you she has banned television from her home and her children are incredibly self-reliant and creative because of it. You reassure yourself that your children don't watch that much television either; they're too busy playing video games.

Your friend sews Halloween costumes for her children. She creates homemade Christmas ornaments with them. And she throws elaborate birthday parties for them. You can barely sew on a button. The only Christmas ornaments you have are the ones your kids haven't broken yet. And the last birthday party you hosted involved a store-bought cake, no party favors and a broken arm.

Another parent tells you about the relaxing weekend her family had. If pressed, you'd have to say your family life is a little like a zoo with the lions loose: a lot of running around and screaming going on.

And worst of all, you can't help but feel like it's *all your fault*.

Remember, things aren't always what they seem. Nod smugly as other parents carry on about their child's many talents and accomplishments and think to yourself, "You're embezzling from the Little League, aren't you?"

And remind yourself that the age at which your children are potty-trained does not correlate with how many soccer goals they'll make some day. And how many soccer goals they make will not relate in any way to the GPA they'll earn in college. And their GPA will have nothing to do with how often they'll visit you in your old age. And isn't that what you're after anyway?

This book is for all you Imperfect Parents out there, all you mothers and fathers who feel you're never good enough. You're not alone. You're better than you know and better than your children will tell you—until they grow up and have kids of their own.

A Brief Explanation about How This Book Works
(Or Doesn't):

One of the trickiest things about putting together a collection of parenting essays is that my son Isaac has been different ages at different times. This is normal. I have too. But it makes writing about parenting difficult. I have divided the book based on categories rather than ages, so those who don't read this note may assume I have many children. I do not. I have one, who, now that I've published a book about parenting, probably wishes I'd had many more.

I
Postpartum Preoccupation

Picking the Bathroom Lock and Other Lessons of Motherhood

You can put a child to bed, but you can't make him sleep; you can set food before him, but you can't make him eat; and you can lead him to the potty, but you can't make him go.

As we near Mother's Day, I can't help but ponder these and other bits of wisdom I've gained since I became a mother four years ago. Perhaps my sharing them will benefit other new parents—but probably not. Still, here goes:

I've learned that items which have survived countless moves, violent acts of nature and even burglaries can be shattered in seconds at the hands of a toddler. And I've learned that young children will never use crayons on the furniture again—once they've tried permanent markers.

I've learned that toddlers can watch the same movie 700 times and never tire of it. (What do they think? It's going to end differently?) And I've learned it doesn't matter that they can't read; they still know when you're leaving out parts of the story.

Since I became a mom, I've acquired some new skills too. I can now do with one hand everything I once did with two. I can make up a bedtime story. I can clean up almost anything without gagging. And I can pick the lock on our bathroom door.

I've learned to be more patient. My record is answering 41 "why questions" before screaming, "Because I said so, that's why!"

And I think I'm more flexible too. It doesn't matter how late I am; if my son Isaac just threw up, I deal with it.

I've learned to lower my expectations about pretty much everything, including the way I dress, the way my house looks and the food I eat. I've learned to eat hot dogs—and not just at the ballpark. I can now step over rubbish on the floor without so much as a glance back. And I've gone to work with my stretch pants on backwards. (There was a time I wouldn't even wear stretch pants, let alone backwards.)

Had I never been a mother I would never have known about sippy cups and wet wipes. I would never have learned how dangerous it is to share pizza with a child while wearing a dry-clean-only dress or how, with the right pressure, a one-ounce packet of salad dressing can get really good coverage in a crowded restaurant.

Had I never been a mom, I would never have learned that a solo trip to the grocery store could be such a treat. I would never have known where my church keeps their carpet sweeper and where the bathroom is located in every business within a five-mile radius of my home.

And finally, had I never been a mother, I would never have learned how one little hug from a child can make a mother forgive and forget a multitude of misdeeds.

Unfortunately, my son has learned that too.

J.K. Rowling, Julia Roberts and Me

Julia Roberts and I have a lot in common. Or maybe a little in common. Okay, one thing in common. We both came to motherhood later in life. Oh, wait; there is one more thing. She's been in some movies, and I've seen some of the movies she's been in.

Just like Julia, I had a baby when I was 36 years old. It wasn't so bad; I was in as good a shape as many 35-year-olds. But not as good as Julia. (I think I can be on a first name basis with her since we have something so important in common.)

And I'm not ashamed of being an older mother. There are certain advantages: At crowded school programs, younger parents let you take the last remaining chair. By the time you're a grandmother, you're accustomed to being called one. And you join a crowd of the rich and famous: Jane Seymour, Geena Davis, Madonna, J.K. Rowling and Susan Sarandon all had babies long after the old biological clock needed new batteries.

There are some advantages to being the children of older parents too. While it is true that we tend to hold the storybooks at arm's length when we read to our kids, we can tolerate the noise level that comes with children better because we can't actually hear it.

Rocking sick babies in the middle of the night isn't hard for some middle-aged parents. We're up all night anyway.

A few years down the road, older mothers will go through perimenopause around the same time our sons go through puberty. Then we can compare moustaches.

And finally, when our kids are grown we'll be retired and free to visit them every weekend. They'll like that, won't they?

But I have to admit that some of the other perceived advantages of older parenthood are myths. For example, some people make the irrational claim that having children when you're older will somehow keep you young. Colic keeps no one young, not even the baby.

There are those who argue that older parents have more of the maturity and wisdom necessary to raise children. But maturity and wisdom are not givens. I waited and waited and I finally had to go ahead without them.

Another common misconception is that older parents are more financially stable than their younger counterparts. While this is certainly true for Madonna and J. K. Rowling, for the rest of us any extra financial resources we have available for our children probably came from robbing our retirement accounts.

There are also some myths about the benefits of having children when you're a child yourself, the main one being that you'll be able to enjoy your middle years childfree. This is only true for those whose kids don't move back home. We older parents will never have to worry about that; there won't be room for them in assisted living.

My friend, who became a mom in her twenties, says she believes older mothers experience more awe and amazement at their children than those who become mothers at a younger age do. And I think there is something to that. Of course, it may not be awe and amazement at all; it may be shock.

Postpartum Preoccupation

What has become of me? I walked into a convenience store, filled a cup at the soda fountain and walked out—without paying. I swear I've never stolen anything in my life. I simply forgot. Really. It's just that my mind was already at work, but my body was still walking out of the store. It didn't help that it was walking pretty darn fast.

It's not like me. There was a time in my life when I never forgot a meeting or missed a deadline. I sent birthday cards to all my family and friends, including those I hadn't seen since second grade. I even had Isaac on his due date.

And that's when everything changed.

An experienced working mother told me not to worry. She said absentmindedness is a natural byproduct of motherhood. With all that a mom has to do, she can't possibly remember everything. Certain less important things—like her middle name and her address—just have to fall by the wayside.

I suppose that could explain why I put wet clothes in the dryer and forgot to turn it on. Or why I put the salt in the refrigerator and the eggs in the cupboard—the bathroom cupboard. Maybe it explains why I ran to the grocery store for one item and came home with fifteen—but not the one I went for. It might explain why I left my car door wide open on Sunday. (Good thing there were no car thieves in church that day.)

It may even explain why I have, not once but many times, driven right past my destination. There's no telling how far I would have gone had my Japanese exchange student not reminded me I'd just missed my turn. (Keep in mind, he's from another country.)

Maybe the fact that I have too much on my mind can justify all of that. But is it really enough to explain why I left my car running for two hours while I sat in my office working?

"Of course it is," said my friend. Then she related how a mutual acquaintance and fellow working mother had taken an airline flight and left her car running in the airport parking lot. She didn't even discover what she'd done—or rather, not done—until she came back a week later to a dead battery and an empty gas tank.

It's reassuring to know I'm not alone. Working mothers everywhere face the same malady. (By the way, the term "working mother" is redundant. The dictionary definition of a "mother," working or otherwise, is "one who sits down only to use the bathroom and even then she's interrupted.") I know a working mother who went out dancing with a diaper pin attached to her evening gown, proving that moms weren't any less distracted back in the days of cloth diapers. And I know more than one mother who has worn her clothes inside out. I know a working mom who paid for fast food in the drive through, then drove away without it. And I know a working mom who actually forgot Mother's Day—and was not reminded by her family.

Without a doubt moms have far too much on our minds. We must remember which days are swim days and which are gymnastics days, which days are meeting days and which are deadline days, which days are paydays and which are pay-the-daycare days. We must never leave home without a selection of snacks, our cell phone, a box of wet wipes and a packet of tissues.

We must arrange entertainment, transportation, medical appointments and meals for the family and, depending on our job, possibly for customers as well. It's a lot like juggling only there are more balls in the air. More on the ground too.

Working mothers, and indeed all mothers, have so much going on and so little time to think about it all that it's truly amazing they don't forget more. Miraculously, they always manage to remember what's truly important. I take that back. I do know two working mothers who drove away without their children.

Let Them Eat Cake—or Crayons

Unlike some children, my toddler is not the least bit finicky. He'll eat almost anything—provided he finds it on the floor. As luck would have it, there's usually something there for him.

Good thing, because he won't eat anything that's broken, unless he's the one who broke it. He won't eat anything he loved so much last week that I went out and bought a case of it. And he won't eat anything at all in front of someone who has just told me he is too thin.

Intellectually I know my son will eat when he needs to and won't when he doesn't. But as his mother it's my job to worry, and I'm darn good at it.

If, like me, you need reassurance that a child you know isn't starving just feet away from a full refrigerator, you might try the following:

I've been known to count peas, corn and macaroni before and then again after a meal. I've attempted to reassemble mauled pizza, sandwiches and toast after Isaac is finished eating, all in order to determine if he has eaten anything at all. Quite often the answer is no; he has not. He has merely toyed with his food and with me as well.

Because most often a child's food is beyond any hope of reassembly, a better method is to actually weigh what you plan to serve. Then when the meal is over, combine what is left on the plate with what you sweep off the floor, scrape off the walls and remove from his or her hair. Subtract the weight of all of this from the original total to get a rough estimate of actual intake. If your child is like mine, you will probably find that he or she has netted very little from the gross, "gross" being the operative word here.

If after you have weighed, counted and reassembled nearly unrecognizable food items, you discover that your child's total intake for the entire day was an orange slice, a tablespoon of green Play-doh and a dust bunny, you might try taking him or her to one of those family friendly restaurants that are kind enough to provide drawing paper and color crayons before the meal arrives. There is something about eating out that improves my son's appetite. At the very least, he fills up on crayons.

You might also try disguising food with nutrient-dense condiments such as ranch dressing, jelly and catsup, which, in case you're wondering, does count as a vegetable when you eat it by the spoonful, as Isaac does (except that he doesn't always use the spoon). But be aware, toddlers have an amazing ability to eat cream cheese off a bagel and butter off toast without taking even one crumb with it.

Occasionally a toddler will manage to eat actual food—before it hits the floor. If you want to increase the chances of this happening, put him or her in a cart full of groceries you haven't paid for yet.

My son once ate a half a pound of grapes—dirt, pesticides and all—while I was shopping. I didn't even try to stop him. If he wants to eat, I feed him. It could be weeks before he feels so inclined again. Plus eating grapes kept him too busy to stock my cart with groceries that weren't on my list. I did confess to the clerk that she should charge me for more grapes than it appeared I had. She said, "Oh, he couldn't have eaten that many."

Oh yes, he could have. He was probably really hungry. He hadn't eaten anything but ranch dressing for three days.

Are You Going to Eat That?

Children are fattening! I mean raising them—not eating them. For one thing, parents don't have a lot of time to exercise, partly because we spend so much time watching our children exercise. And while jumping up and down, yelling "Go the *other* way!" burns calories, it doesn't burn as many as getting out on the field and running the wrong way ourselves.

Besides that, couples who become parents see a gradual transformation in their diets from "real food," which is lower in calories and higher in nutrients, to "kid food" which is higher in calories and nearly devoid of nutrients. But what "kid food" lacks in nutrition it more than makes up for in carbohydrates and fat grams.

Before we know it, macaroni and cheese becomes a staple, "fruit snacks" replace real fruit and our freezer is full of fish sticks and hot dogs. Children love these "foods" and they can be eaten in the car on the way to the game—except for maybe the macaroni and cheese.

Finally, many an excess parental pound is packed on because parents are willing to eat what our children have left behind. The following example of lunch at my house illustrates how this can become a problem:

Turkey sandwich on whole wheat bread with light mayonnaise: 250 calories

Apple: 80 calories

Skim Milk: 90 calories

Total: 420 calories.

Not bad. I even abstain from the brownies—360 calories each—that I baked for my son's dessert. (Understand this is merely for illustration purposes. I never bake anything, and if I ever do, I won't abstain.)

Then as I clean up the lunch mess (and it is a mess), I absentmindedly consume the mauled remains of my son's sandwich (100 calories), the flattened remnants of his brownie (300 calories), and his leftover 2 percent milk (100 calories) with brownie crumbs in it (3 calories).

I have now devoured 923 calories, 503 of which I don't even "count." And this is just lunch; I still have his snacks and supper to finish.

Why would a parent eat food that has been mangled by dirty little fingers? I think it starts innocently when a new mother lets her baby lick the ice cream off her spoon or sip from her drink. Blinded by love and fatigue, she hardly notices the slobber. A boundary is crossed and before she knows it she's gnawing on a leftover pizza crust.

And another thing: parents don't like to waste food. Let me give you an example taken from real life—mine. I bought Isaac a box of four miniature cinnamon rolls at a fast food restaurant. He ate one. I had never before been tempted to buy miniature cinnamon rolls for myself, let alone eat them. But rather than waste them, I ate the remaining three. They were better than I thought they'd be. The next time we were at that restaurant, I ordered TWO boxes of miniature cinnamon rolls, one for him and one for me. He ate two of the four in his package. I ate all four of mine—and the rest of his.

Sometimes a parent eats off her child's plate for the same reason a dog chews on a bone: because it's there. Say you're having a picnic at the park. Your children take two bites of chicken, declare themselves full and dash off to the monkey bars where they will burn hundreds of calories. You sit and watch, enjoying the fresh air, the sound of your children's laughter and the rest of their lunch.

What can be done—short of not having children (though if you're reading this, it's probably too late for that)? First, when you're tempted by thriftiness, remind yourself that while throwing food away might be a waste, it's also a waste sitting on your…uh…waist.

Second, pay attention. Actually look at that thing you're about to put in your mouth. Doing this has the added advantage of ruining your appetite for anything else you might be tempted to eat the rest of the day.

Into the Mouths of Babes

Recently in a restaurant, I saw a very large man threaten a very small boy to clean his plate—or else. When the child didn't oblige, the father got really tough—he cleaned the plate for his son. It occurred to me that here in overweight America, some of us may not be qualified to teach our children about a healthy lifestyle.

Not only that, we might actually be able to learn a few things about healthy eating from young children. Granted, they make a few mistakes when it comes to dining, not the least of which is eating directly off the floor. Forget the three second rule; my son will eat it after three days.

Children eat with their mouths open. They lick the serving spoon, then put it back in the bowl. They eat non-finger foods with their fingers—tapioca pudding, for example. And they can survive for weeks on one food group. Quite often it's the condiment group.

Still, young children have a few eating habits that I, for one, would do well to imitate. For starters, if it doesn't taste good to them kids won't eat it. We adults will eat anything. I know this because I've fed a lot of people a lot of things at my house. How many times have you said at my house or elsewhere, "This really isn't very good." Then you ate it anyway.

A young child would never do that. She would quickly remove the offensive food item from her mouth, display it in the palm of her hand to everyone at the table and say, "This is yucky." While this approach needs some polish, it does save calories.

Until we teach them to, children never feel they must eat everything on their plate—though they do feel they must touch everything on their plate. Someday when they are plump like us, a wise weight-loss counselor will assure them there is no law that says they must clean their plate. He or she will go on to say that no matter what anyone has told them, eating after they are full will not ease the pain their ancestors endured during the Depression. Gradually they will learn to leave food on their plates, all the while telling their own children to clean theirs.

On a related note, children eat only when they're hungry. We adults eat when we're sad. Children weep, wail and blubber, which burns calories. We eat when we're happy. Children skip and bounce, which burns calories. We eat when we're mad. Children throw fits, which burn *many* calories.

And children can actually spoil their dinner. Oh, that I could spoil my dinner! I tell my son, "I know you're hungry, but if you eat that cookie, you won't be able to eat your dinner." Then, as soon as he's out of the room, I eat the cookie. Then I eat my dinner.

Young children take their time eating. We tell them, "Hurry up and eat." But by the time they've tunneled through their mashed potatoes and lined up their corn kernels, we've eaten our third helping and eliminated any possibility of their having seconds. Eventually, in self-defense they will learn to hurry up. Then someday when they're attending a weight loss support group, they will be counseled to slow down when they eat and to enjoy what they're doing—though not necessarily by lining up their corn kernels.

Finally, young children exercise. In the unlikely event that they do actually ingest a calorie, they exercise enough to burn it off—usually before they've left the dinner table.

You Can Lead a Child to Potty but You Can't Make Him Go

My son was born exactly on his due date. I took that as a sign that he would always be right on time. I should have taken into consideration the fact that his due date was April Fool's Day.

As dust collected in the potty-chair, my husband and I tried to remain hopeful. Like all young children, our son could sense our naive optimism and he quickly learned to use it to his advantage. A child who can't even say the word "manipulate" somehow knows he can escape a church service, a restaurant, a car seat or a bed simply by saying five little words—"I have to go potty"—even if he doesn't, and even if he wouldn't know what to do if you gave him the opportunity.

During the potty training ordeal new parents discover it really does take a village to raise a child. The village thinks so anyway. There are a few kind people who step forward to reassure the anxious parent. "Don't worry, I've never once seen anyone who's not potty trained graduate from high school…or walk down the aisle…or have children of their own." These words are small comfort to a parent who's had a recurring nightmare about an untrained eighth grader.

Far more of the feedback on potty training is even less comforting. Before their child is even walking, new parents begin to hear legends of mythical pottiers. One soon realizes that denial and poor memory surround the topic of potty training. After hearing countless potty stories, the new parent begins to see a pattern: the longer it's been since training was an issue, the earlier the child in question was allegedly trained.

The new parent is also bound to hear a great deal of advice on the subject of methodology. Any number of people told me that as soon as their child was 18 months old, they began sitting him or her on the potty every hour. I tried this for a short time. I sat beside my son and read him inspirational stories, focusing on several about Noah's Ark (you know, the flood).

It didn't take me long to see this method wasn't for us. My sincere belief is that if you put anyone on a toilet every hour on the hour, all day long, eventually something will happen. The question is who would be trained, him to go potty or me to watch the clock?

Another method, which I liked better, involved rewarding each successful attempt. M&Ms seemed to be the reward of choice so I stocked up. This method didn't work at my house not because it wasn't a good idea, but because the trainer kept eating the trainee's rewards.

In the end I think it was just plain my son's idea. That and what my daycare provider cleverly refers to as "pee-er pressure." Beyond that, the only hard and fast rule I see in the potty training game is this: the child will be trained when the child decides to be trained. In other words, you can lead a child to potty but you can't make him go.

And now that it's all behind us, I can look at potty training as a valuable learning experience. Had I never been through it I would never have learned the locations of every bathroom at every business in town. And I would never have heard those encouraging words after leaving a restroom myself, "Good job, Mommy!"

Finding Peace in Play Land

The play area at a fast food restaurant is a lot like a blender with the lid off. Why do I come here?

It's not to feed my son, that's for sure. I beg, plead, insist and demand that he eat, and after two bites he says, "I'm full" with such sincerity that I believe him. Then he takes off to play. I sit still and eat my meal and half of his. He's the one burning calories; I'm the one eating them. No, I don't come here to feed my son.

Nor do I come here for the toys that come with the kids' meals. I don't want more toys in our home. My son does. He wants them desperately—for ten minutes. He tears open the toy du jour, plays with it long enough to smear it with ketchup, and then forgets about it. I won't be able to forget about it. I'll remember it the minute I step on it later tonight. No, I don't go to the play area for the toys.

And I certainly don't go to the play area to spend time with Isaac. He disappears the minute we enter and only comes back occasionally for a sip of his drink. Not only that, our relationship is damaged a little each time we leave the play area. It would be lovely if when it was time to go, he'd say sweetly, "You're the best mom in the world for bringing me here. But now I see it's time to go."

Instead, I know that leaving the play area will involve me yelling at Isaac while he crawls through a large tube stretching across the ceiling over my head. I've learned never to call him unless he's within grabbing distance. That's because I'm a bit claustrophobic and my behind is larger than a five-year-old's. That makes retrieval nearly impossible and he knows it. No, bonding is not why we come here.

So why do I come to the fast food play area? It's simple. I'm not proud to admit this, but I get more time to myself when I'm surrounded by fifty screaming children playing with each other than when I'm alone with one who wants to play with me.

Decisions about Sick Kids Make Parents Ill

Parents of a sick child have difficult decisions to make quickly. Do I keep him home from school or not? Do I take her to the doctor or not? Does the dosage amount on the medicine bottle allow for what he spits back at me or not?

The child is no help to the parent making these decisions. Ask her if she should go to the doctor and the answer will always be, "*No!*" Ask him if he should stay home from school and the answer will always be, "*Yes!*"—unless there's a field trip planned that day.

So let's consider each of these questions carefully:

Do I keep him/her home from school? If I stay home with my son, there's a good chance that in a few hours he'll be begging me to play baseball. I would be a very bad employee if I take the day off to play baseball, now wouldn't I? (And anyway, I really don't like to play baseball.)

He's going to school.

On the other hand, if I take him to school there's a good chance that the principal's office will call me at 10 o'clock imploring me to come get him because he threw up all over his teacher's desk. I would be a bad mother if I took a truly sick child to school, now wouldn't I?

He's staying home.

But then again, will the child, who has barely been able to lift his head for a sip of cold water, come alive the minute I call my office? And while I'm on the phone telling my boss, "I'm keeping my son home because he's sick," will he holler, "Mom, let's wrestle"?

It could happen.

I recall being on the phone with the president of a local organization, telling her that the doctor had just diagnosed Isaac with pneumonia. Consequently I would be unable to make a speech to her group that day. He chose that moment to run by doing his finest impression of a fire truck. "Must be walking pneumonia," she said sarcastically.

"No," I said, "it's running, jumping and screaming pneumonia." He collapsed into a heap moments later—but not until after I hung up the telephone.

He's going to school!

Maybe.

The second question the parent must answer is, "Do I take him to the doctor?" This decision is not as easy to make as one might think. Will the doctor say, "It will have to run its course"? And will medical professionals snicker and whisper "hysterical mother" as I leave the clinic?

I'm giving it one more day.

On the other hand, nights are eternal with a sick child. I recall a particular ear infection. It was 3 a.m. and Mickey Mouse was on the TV. My son was curled up in my lap; I held a warm washcloth to his ear. And I remember thinking, the whole town is asleep and I'm watching Mickey Mouse conduct the William Tell Overture. How did it come to this? I didn't take him to the doctor, that's how.

He's going to the doctor.

But then again, children punish their parents for every time they stood by and did nothing while a medical professional poked and prodded. That's why a child who hasn't moved in days can summon the strength to dismantle a waiting room. And a child whose lack of fluid intake has his parents worried sick about dehydration will sweetly ask for a drink of water the minute they're in the doctor's office.

I'll give it one more day and see how he's doing tomorrow.
Definitely.
I think.

Dead People at the Daycare

Even when you're blessed with a quality daycare and wonderful babysitters, as we were, childcare can be traumatic—for parents. Kids do fine with it.

To manage, parents must have a great deal of trust in their childcare providers—which we did. They must also have honest, open communication with the provider because whenever two or more children are gathered together, issues will arise—strange rashes, bite marks and new vocabulary words.

Worse are the mysterious stories told by children who aren't yet able to communicate. One day when my son was around four years old, he refused to go to the daycare. This was unusual for him, but not nearly as unusual as his reason. He said he didn't want to go because of the dead people in the bathroom. Being fairly certain there were no dead people in the bathroom at the daycare, or in any other room for that matter, I asked him if maybe the dead people were dolls. He was adamant that they were not dolls. He said there were three or four of them, they were about his size, and the teachers took their heads off and put them in the bathroom. Wow. I wouldn't want to go to that daycare either.

I promised my son I would investigate and if there really were dead people in the bathroom, naturally he would not have to stay at that daycare nor, I imagine, would any of the other children.

Thanks to the excellent relationship and outstanding communication we had with our day care provider, I felt comfortable being upfront about the situation. When we arrived at the daycare, I told the first teacher we met as delicately as I could that my son was afraid of the dead people they kept in the bathroom. She laughed a little nervously, then she suggested gently that my son had an overactive imagination. Admittedly he did, and still does, have an active imagination, but at four he had not yet dreamt up homicide.

The second teacher understood immediately. She went into the bathroom and came out carrying a body. I'm joking. Actually she was carrying a small dummy used for CPR training—complete with head.

Trust and good communication are also necessary when a babysitter is coming to the house. We had many trustworthy babysitters. But there were a few who took the fun out of an evening out. The minute she got in our door one babysitter asked us how much we were going to pay her because she was saving for a cell phone.

I'm not naïve. I was once a babysitter myself and I know that all babysitters have three questions on their minds: how much are these people going to pay me, what time do the kids go to bed, and what kind of snacks do they have in this house? Still coming right out and asking does nothing to establish trust.

One of our babysitters invited her boyfriend over to cuddle on the couch while Isaac watched television. Another invited his friends over to skateboard on our driveway. Isaac told us the next day that the babysitter's friends hadn't been very nice to him, so he'd gone into the house and locked them out until they all went home. The babysitter had the good sense to stay until Isaac let him back in.

Fortunately we had open, honest communications with all of these babysitters. We didn't even have to say very much. We just didn't invite them back.

Will Sweetiekins Give the Steak Knifey Back to Daddy?

New parents plead with their babies to "talk." A couple of years later, they beg their preschoolers to *stop* talking. A few more years and they implore their preteen to talk.

"What did you do in school today?"

"Nothing." Or more precisely, "Nuthin."

Parents of young children encourage, beseech and even force them to talk on the telephone to grandparents and aunts and uncles. Then the day comes when they have to wrestle the telephone away from their teenager to call 911.

While these changes may be troublesome, they are natural steps in the development of parent/child communication. And there are many others. The grammar and pronunciation of new parents evolve. "Is him hungwee?" "Her the smartest baby in the whole, wide world." And, "Momma sweepy after yittle babykins awake all @#$!%^&* night."

New parents begin to add unusual endings to common words, as in "nighty-night" and "beddy-bye." They start using synonyms not found in any thesaurus. Trains become "choo-choos" and injuries become "boo-boos." Even the voices of new parents change from those of adults to those of adults on helium.

Parents of babies and toddlers unconsciously stop using pronouns. It's never, "I'm going to kiss you." It's, "Mommy kiss baby doll" or "Give the steak knifey back to Daddy."

Thankfully the parent eventually begins to use pronouns again, and with a new vigor, as in, "If I told you once I've told you a thousand times...."

Parents of toddlers and elementary school children respond to every request their children make—and there are many—with, "What do you say?" This is meant to instill the habitual use of "please" and "thank you." Unfortunately the question becomes so automatic that parents may occasionally slip up and use it on other people's children, including full-grown ones, as in the following exchange:

"Hey lady! Move your car!"

"Now, what do you say?"

Parents instinctively pave the way for their offspring to learn to spell by spelling every word they don't want the child to understand. One day they find out just how well this works when the child spells a few choice words for Grandma.

Similarly parents help their children learn to count by frequently counting out loud themselves. "Do I have to count? One . . . .two . . . *three*." This would be more educational, but not as effective as a discipline tool, if we counted higher: "...98...99...100. Now do what I told you to do—whatever it was."

We could spend an entire essay discussing the evolution of the word "no" in the parent/child relationship. Parents of young children say "no" often and with feeling. "No! Don't touch that hot stove!" "No! Don't eat kitty's food." "No! Don't wash teddy in the toilet!" While the child doesn't necessarily learn to obey, he or she does learn to say, "No!"

The next phase of "no" training goes like this: The child asks for something. The parent says, "No." The child asks again. The parent says, "No," this time with more enthusiasm. The child asks again, but in a different way. The parent says, "No" even more loudly. This goes on until one of the parties has a temper tantrum, usually the parent.

Unbelievably, after all the years of "no" training, there still comes a time when the parent must teach their teenager to "just say no."

But never fear! All of these stages in parent/child communication are part of a natural progression to a moment when both sides will begin to speak to each other as equals. It's too bad that by that time the parent won't be able to hear anymore.

II
Take It Outside!
You're Driving Me Nuts

Put the Gun Down and Come Eat Your Breakfast

I'm awakened by five young toughs carrying weapons. I'm groggy and confused but unafraid—maybe because they're rubbing their eyes and wearing their jammies. Besides, there aren't enough weapons to go around, so one of them is carrying a clipboard.

It's the morning after a birthday sleepover and the toys and games remind me: boy play is goofy. Having been a girl myself, I can say without a doubt that girl play is also goofy—or at least it was when I was playing. It's just goofy in different ways.

Even boy toys are weird. While many toys marketed to girls are stupid and sappy, many toys marketed to boys are stupid and creepy, especially the dolls. And yes, boys have dolls; they just don't call them dolls. And if you know what's good for you, you won't call them dolls either. You'll call them "action figures." But they're dolls nonetheless; they're just ugly dolls.

Girls' dolls talk. Boys' dolls make strange beeping noises. Girls' dolls wear gobs of makeup and have retractable hair. Boys' dolls wear shields and have retractable heads.

And then there's the weaponry. It's almost a cliché that if parents swear off toy weapons, their sons will shoot with bananas. Or tennis shoes. Or toothbrushes. After a while you hardly notice that cuddled up next to your son's Cookie Monster is a plastic grenade and a triple action machine gun.

I don't know about girls, but boys are intensely competitive. As I often am, I was recently called to settle a serious argument between my son and his friend: can a sword block a bullet? I have no expertise in weaponry, but I do know a thing or two about diplomacy. And I knew that a definite answer would have one boy mad at me and both boys mad at each other. "It depends on the sword, the bullet and how far they are apart. But it's certainly possible," I said with a nod to one boy. "But not likely," I added with a nod to the other. They walked away from me, each saying, "I told you so."

Boys take up the entire house. If there's a war going on, as there often is, there will be collateral damage in every room. I've even found army men in my purse, which can be embarrassing at the checkout counter.

Boys have a great sense of fairness—especially when they think they're being treated unfairly. And they generally play by the rules, which is harder than it sounds when you consider how often the rules change.

During a recent spine-tingling playdate in our home, the list of items that could be destroyed by toxic waste grew faster than an oil spill. "You said toxic waste can't destroy a robot."

"It can when the robot is made of...titanium."

"Mine isn't! It's made of...aluminum...and plastic."

"Even worse!"

"But his protective shield is on."

"I turned it off with my...toxic laser beam."

"You can't do that. Only I can do that with my...protective shield switcher."

"I just did it."

Parenting experts would agree that intervening in such a debate is unwise. Children must be allowed to work out their own disagreements in order to become mature adults who can cooperatively settle disagreements about toxic laser beams and aluminum robots.

But sometimes even the best of parents is tempted to chime in with some great pearl of wisdom like, "Take it outside! You're driving me nuts!"

Here Comes Santa Claus (Oh, Goodie)

My son may not agree, but I think he needs more toys like Bill Gates needs more money. I land on Legos when I fall into bed at night. I step on little green army men when I drag out of bed in the morning. I gave Mr. Potato Head away years ago and I still find his body parts all over my house.

All day long I shove aside, stumble over, pick up and swear at toys. It might not be good for my son to hear that.

The childless and parents of grown children will say naively, "Well, stop buying toys." But modern parents don't have to buy toys; toys find us. Often they're given to us by the childless and parents of grown children.

Plus today's children get toys as prizes every time they sell fundraising items, which is often. Toys are an incentive for young salespeople. But they are a disincentive for parents, who are the encouragers, motivators, drivers. We'd prefer they received a commission. That way they could reimburse us for the gas used in their sales calls.

And of course, restaurants serve toys with their meals and are very popular because of it. I've tried this at home but to no effect, maybe because I was serving used toys.

Even dentists give small toys to their young patients. Why can't they just pass out candy like they used to?

Before we know it, toys have taken over our home like dandelions on our lawn. As parents we know that quality toys serve a purpose. They allow kids to play creatively and keep them occupied so we can read the newspaper. But we can't help but fear we're raising little materialists who think it's normal to get a new toy every other day.

That's why I'm unveiling my new six-step plan to decrease the number of toys in the home.

1. First of all, don't have children. If it's too late for that, skip to number 2.

2. Just before Christmas, instruct your children to give away an agreed-upon number of old toys. I'm thinking 50 to 100, though getting them to agree to that might be difficult. Try appealing to their higher motives by telling them that their beloved toys will be in the hands of less fortunate children who will love them as much as they did. If that doesn't work, appeal to their baser motives; remind them that Christmas is coming and they need to make room. If that doesn't work, do it yourself while they're sleeping.

3. Encourage friends and relatives to give functional gifts, such as money for the college fund or socks and underwear, which are always a hit with children.

4. Try re-gifting. During the frenzy of opening gifts, some toys are quickly shoved aside, still in their packaging, as the child reaches for the next gift. Snatch a few of these and set them aside for the next birthday party your child is invited to. Later they may ask where these toys are. This is a teachable moment, and that's why you should lie. Say in your sternest parent voice, "With as many toys as you have, it's no wonder you can't find them."

5. Refuse kids' meal toys at fast food restaurants. You could even order them an adult meal and eat their leftovers.

6. There are certain toys you must ban entirely from your home. These include toys that promote violence or disrespect and any that say anywhere on the packaging, "Collect all twelve!"

Changing Socks Barbie

Some would say it was the blight on an otherwise perfect childhood, but I never owned a Barbie doll. I had some Barbie wannabes (namely Midge and Penny, whom I still think of fondly), but no actual Barbie.

My only child is a son. Isaac's doll collection consists of a fireman, a soldier and some unattractive action figures that don't quite live up to the name "doll." I know nothing of Barbie.

So when the mother of a little girl on my Christmas list assured me that a Barbie would do nicely, I naively thanked her for making it easy for me. I began my search for a Barbie thinking it would be over faster than it would take the child to open my gift.

How could I have known there are more Barbies than Jell-O varieties? Should I choose the Barbie Royal Romance set or Barbie pushing Krissy in a baby carriage? Should I go with Bead Blast Barbie or Hula Hair Barbie? What about Olympic Skater Barbie, Soccer Barbie or Twirling Ballerina Barbie?

In a daze I wandered out of the Barbie aisle into that of the less well known dolls. I saw dolls that could talk, walk and laugh. I saw a doll whose hair could be pulled out and reeled back in to change the length. If I'd had a doll like that when I was a child, I might not have cut the hair on my sister's doll. (She noticed immediately, despite—or maybe because of—my efforts to conceal my work with Scotch tape.)

I saw dollhouses as nice as any home I've lived in, and only slightly smaller. They brought back memories of my own dollhouse, a wooden box with a hinged lid, which, when open, became a magnificent split-level home. I had miniature dolls, but all from different sets. Consequently, the mother doll (Debbie) had a baby (Baby) as large as she was.

I saw beautiful baby doll carriages and was reminded of the time I pushed my own doll carriage off the bed in an effort to determine if the wheels would go around in mid-air. I can't remember now if they did or not, but I do know that, once they hit the ground, they stopped going around at all.

Back again in the Barbie aisle, I came across the Barbie clothing line. Barbie has more clothes than Midge, Penny and me put together. I designed my dolls' clothing using socks. I'd cut off the upper part of a sock and make two arm holes in it. The style didn't show off their Barbie-like figures very well and the collar was never quite right, but I could make the dresses whatever length I wanted, from mini to evening gown. Imagine argyle evening wear. Unfortunately I never learned to do sleeves, so no matter how cold the weather, Midge and Penny always went sleeveless. Though most people would not have been so kind, my parents considered my design efforts creative—except when I used new socks.

In the end I left the toy store with nothing but a few returning childhood memories and a renewed appreciation for gift certificates. Later I asked the mother of the little girl who is not getting a Barbie from me, "Why couldn't Spring in Tokyo Barbie just change clothes to become Birthday Wishes Barbie?"

"Blasphemy," said my friend. "Could Glamour Barbie have any credibility at all if she doubled as Bowling Champ Barbie? And would you trust Pilot Barbie if, in her off time, she was Tie-Dye Barbie? Barbie has had more than 80 careers, from astronaut to paleontologist. She's quite an achiever."

Where I work we'd call her a job hopper. But I suppose I'm just jealous. Barbie and I are nearly the same age and I haven't done nearly as well for myself. She's aged better too. Midge and Penny, on the other hand, still look marvelous. And as I recall, they also had a number of exciting professions. And for them it was as easy as changing socks.

Why It's Impossible to Clean a Child's Bedroom

In order to assist a child of any age to clean his/her room, a parent should have a great deal of patience, a dose of understanding—and a large trash bag placed just out of sight.

One encounters many challenges in undertaking this job, the main one being how attached children get to their toys, even the ones they forgot they had. You may think they're no longer interested in items they acquired when they were younger. They may think so too—until you suggest they part with them. Suddenly particular toys are not only special, they're heirlooms to be passed on to their own children one day.

The second problem is the sheer number of toys in the modern child's bedroom. Today's kids receive toys and trinkets for everything they do—eating out, selling popcorn and overpriced cookie dough, even going to the dentist. They have birthday parties with 12 guests who bring 12 useless items … I mean, gifts. And they inherit hand-me-down toys from children whose parents are better at getting their kids to give them up.

The third issue is that many toys come in millions of pieces. We could build a room onto our home with all the Legos Isaac has. And if we ever do we'll use it for toy storage.

Finally, even older children may not have a clear understanding of what "cleaning their room" actually means. There may be smelly socks, rotten apple cores and heaps of toys in every corner, but many children believe that the room is clean as long as there's a small space on the bed for them to sleep.

In order to deal with these challenges you must have a strategy. First, put a trash bag and a box for giveaways out of sight in the hallway. Then label some large plastic containers or cardboard boxes with the categories of toys your child has: guns, trucks, jewelry, costumes, dolls, dishes, miscellaneous garbage. I'm kidding. Don't write that. Your child may not even know what "miscellaneous" means yet.

Now clear off and make the bed. This will prevent any sharp objects or perishable food items from winding up under the covers during the next step. Place the labeled containers on the bed and shove everything that is not where it's supposed to be, which is almost everything, into a giant heap in the center of the room. Then light a match. I'm joking. That would be dangerous.

Instead, both you and your child should begin putting each object into its correct container. Stop periodically to ask your child sweetly, "You don't play with this anymore, do you, honey?"

Sometimes she'll agree quickly. If this is the case, put the item in the trash or give-away container quickly without comment. This is very important. You must never say, "Grandma gave you that," or "You used to play with that a lot," or even "Good riddance!" Any of these may cause the child to change her mind.

Most times the child will argue that yes, she does too play with it, even if the item in question is broken, covered in dust bunnies and not missed since it first disappeared under the bed two years ago.

It's very tempting at this point to lose your temper and start dumping toys into the trash bag by the armload, but that wouldn't be fair. Always remember, these are not your belongings. Plus you'll be caught.

You have to be more subtle than that. Fortunately, you have an advantage. Children are easily distracted. One minute they're cleaning, the next they're playing hand ball against the wall or chewing on a pizza crust they found in the corner. This can be very frustrating but don't despair. Just keep filling up the trash bag while they're not looking.

Quality of the Costume Won't Affect the Quantity of the Take

Among my many failings as a mother, add to the list the fact that I've never made my son Isaac a Halloween costume. I've taken him trick-or-treating; I've checked his treats for dangerous tricks. And I've kept him from overdoing it on sweets by helping myself to his treats when he's not looking.

But I've never made a costume. I'm just not the crafty sort. I can sew on a button and stitch up a hem if I absolutely must. But the last thing I sewed with an actual sewing machine was my thumb, and that has a way of inspiring you to look for other hobbies.

It doesn't help that I've never enjoyed wearing costumes myself. When I was growing up my Halloween costumes consisted mostly of those hard plastic masks that stayed on my face only because the elastic string tangled up in my hair.

I dressed up as Charlie Chaplin at some point in my adulthood, but generally I have steadfastly avoided costume parties. Then I found myself in the midst of a bus full of people headed to one while I was visiting a gambling town. It was late October and my husband and I rode the shuttle from our hotel to the casinos downtown. We soon discovered that we were the only ones *not* on the way to a costume party. We looked painfully out of place, though we told everyone we met that we were a young, hip couple dressed as a frumpy, middle-aged couple.

There were a dozen or so Oompa-Loompas, five or six Draculas, a few cowboys and a lot of loose-looking women. Most of the women's costumes would never work for me. It's cold in late October, and a dance hall girl wearing fleece and wool socks doesn't look right.

I have appeared in several theatre productions, but someone far more creative than I am always came up with my costumes. And I had some wardrobe malfunctions during my drama career that may have contributed to my costume phobia. There was the slip that "slipped" during one performance. I had to wiggle and squirm to keep it from landing around my ankles. Not only did this make it hard for me to remember my lines, the audience probably thought I had fleas.

During another play, my leading man was supposed to light the cigarette I held. Neither of us being smokers, we could not get the darn thing to light. I wound up "smoking" an unlit cigarette during an entire scene. Foolish as it looked, this is how I prefer my cigarettes.

I suppose you're thinking that this is a lengthy justification for why I've never had the ambition to create a costume for my only child. But the fact that I haven't made any doesn't mean he hasn't worn any homemade costumes. He once dressed as Inspector Jacques Clouseau from the Pink Panther movies. The idea was his; the trench coat was mine, and it dragged on the ground—a safety no-no and a drycleaner's nightmare.

Fortunately, you can buy costumes and I've bought many of them. My son has been any number of creatures, including Batman, a soldier and a Star Wars clone trooper. What's the big deal anyway? I give candy to anyone brave enough to knock on my door on Halloween night. I think most people do. Near as I can tell, the quality of the costume never affects the quantity of the haul, and isn't that what we're after anyway?

Pink is Camouflage if You're Hiding in a Flowerbed

One of the people I despise most in the world, though we've never met, is the creator of zip-off pants. Zip-off pants, in case you haven't seen them, have zippers at the knees so you can convert them to shorts whenever the spirit moves you. Then you can forget the legs wherever you happened to be when you were so moved.

My six-year-old son owns four pairs of zip-off pants. Actually, that's not quite right. What he has is one pair of zip-off pants and three partial pairs of zip-off pants. One pair has one full leg and one half leg, and one pair is missing both legs. While both of these could be worn as shorts, that would not be very useful in the winter months. The pair that has two legs but no shorts would not be very useful any time of year.

A wise parent purchases several identical pairs of zip-off pants so they can always piece together one entire pair. I'm not a wise parent, so I didn't think of this when I purchased the much-coveted zip-off pants for Isaac. It had not occurred to me that a child who doesn't even like shorts would be so quick to make himself two pairs.

Friends with daughters tell me I'm lucky I have only a son to dress. It is a widely held belief that dressing a daughter is more difficult because girls care more about what they wear. I can't help but be offended by this stereotype since I happen to be a daughter.

And I'm here to tell you boys are also very particular about their clothing. The fact that they will wear the same clothes every day of the week, even if they have to take them out of the dirty clothes hamper to do it, is only a sign that they are too picky to wear anything else.

My son's fashion preferences started to appear when he was still young enough to have what I thought were adorable little sets, like a T-shirt with a cute little truck appliqué and matching pants and a Winnie the Pooh shorts and top set. One day he announced to me that he didn't like what he called "partners." In other words, he didn't like adorable little sets.

Also, he doesn't like button up shirts because the collars annoy him. He prefers that his socks go all the way up to his knees. And he only wants to wear blue jeans or camouflage pants. I tell him camouflage is relative. Pink pants would be considered camouflage if he were hiding in the flowerbed. He remains unconvinced.

A major cause of our fashion battle is my son's physique. If pants fit him around his waist, they're too short. If he were a she, my argument about how short pants are in style might have worked. I told him short pants even have a name; they're called capris. He told me flatly that he does not now, and never will, want to wear capris. Picky, picky, picky.

Fish Hooks Boy

I could tell from the whoops and hollers down by the lake that my seven-year-old had either fallen in or he'd caught a fish. Based on his history of each, I figured Isaac was in the lake.

But as I hurried back I could see he was standing on the shore with a fish dangling from his pole. We danced, did high fives, took pictures and promised to send copies to friends around the globe. Then we put the fish where all fish of its magnitude belong: back in the lake.

He almost kissed it before he tossed it back. It was his first fish, after all. Coincidentally, I'd also had a first that day. I put a worm on his hook. But not just any worm. The label on the container called it and its friends "Giant Canadian Night Crawlers." These were imported worms. Impressive.

But it wasn't my worm that caught the fish. I don't know if it was the agility of the night crawler, the power of the cast or my own ineptitude, but the worm fell off during casting and provided some fish with a safe, imported lunch. (Actually, I do know which it was.) My husband put on the effective worm.

I have fished very little and I've always managed to con someone less squeamish into baiting my hook. I'm uncomfortable causing pain to anything, even a night crawler. Isaac must have inherited a bit of my soft heart. He put the smallest of the worms back into the container because, as he put it, "He's special to me." Apparently the worm that caught the fish was not so special—or so lucky.

You may be thinking that if I'm not comfortable putting a worm on a hook or taking a fish off a hook, I probably wouldn't make much of a big game hunter either. And you would be right. My idea of hunting is checking the grocery store ads for deals on ground beef.

I may not be a fisherman myself, but I see only benefits to my son's interest. Fishing brings out a patient side in my child I've never seen before. And he is, pardon the pun, hooked. The day after we threw that first fish back, we were at the grocery store. I thought we should have something in our refrigerator besides the remaining night crawlers.

My son, ever the helpful shopper, suggested we buy fish. Why not? I headed for the fish sticks. But he led me back to the cooler where the salmon and the halibut and the rest of the real fish are kept. He picked out a trout wrapped in plastic, eyes and all, as he happily pointed out.

What could I do? He wasn't begging for Pop Tarts or potato chips. He held the fish all the way home from the grocery store.

I prepared it as well as I could; admittedly, it may not have been that great. "What do you think?" I asked him during dinner. "It's okay," he said. But then he added that the fish we threw back would probably have tasted better.

Oh yeah. The one that got away. He's going to be a fisherman, all right.

The Ones That Didn't Get Away

I eat fish, but I don't catch fish. Just like I eat cookies, but I don't bake them. Instinctively fish know this about me—that I don't catch them, not that I don't bake cookies.

Isaac knows both. He also knows that I can be worn down by constant pleading and negotiating in the same way a mountain can be worn down by wind and rain—only faster. That's how he finally persuaded me to take him and his friend fishing. He assured me he would never ask for another thing. He told me I could spend the time reading and walking around the lake. He said they would throw back any fish smaller than six inches. I should have noticed they didn't bring a ruler.

I should tell you that I don't know how to clean fish and, as it turns out, neither did they. The real fishermen in their lives have never seen fit to bring home any of the fish they've caught. But there were no real fishermen available—only me, the one in the family who believes fishing is what you do only if you forgot to bring a book to the lake.

I did remember a book, so I spent two glorious hours reading and walking—the calm before the storm. I could see the boys across the lake. I didn't hear any whooping and hollering, which I assumed meant the fish weren't biting. To someone who eats fish but doesn't catch them, two hours seems like a long time to fish without any luck. I didn't care; I was enjoying myself. I honked when it was time to leave, and they started back around the lake without argument. It was all going so well that I decided I might even take them fishing again. I've since changed my mind.

Eventually, they made it back to the car, but what was that? They had three fish on a stringer. The irony was hard to miss: they never bring fish home when they go with real fishermen, but I take them once and they bring home three. They were small and they were dead, but they were fish.

We drove the more than twenty minutes into town with the dead fish wrapped in plastic bags—maybe to show them to real fisherman before we disposed of them. Isaac's friend said he thought he felt them move. I thought that was just wishful thinking—until I saw it myself in my kitchen moments later. In case you're wondering, that's when I changed my mind about taking the boys fishing again.

We had two choices: Put the fish in a bucket and drive them back to the lake to grow up, or learn to clean fish fast. Driving them back seemed like a waste, but so did cleaning them. Let's just say it would give a whole new meaning to the term "petit filet."

While I was pondering these options, the fishermen came up with a third: they put the fish in the bathtub. The fish were happy. The boys were ecstatic. I was not. They thought the fish would make good pets and could live in our bathroom indefinitely. I was concerned about bath time. Besides, while my bathtub may be good habitat for any number of species, fish probably isn't one of them. I repeated my call for options one or two.

We didn't think of Google which nowadays is how you learn to do everything from bake brownies to deliver babies. Instead the boys started making phone calls, leaving me to wonder: with all the real fishermen they apparently knew, how did I get stuck taking them fishing? They did get a few tips by phone, but not what I was hoping for—a house call by an actual fisherperson.

My mother finally came to the rescue. She gave the boys some pointers and the crisis was averted. I was saved a trip to the lake. The boys learned to clean fish. And there are three small ones in my freezer and none in my bathtub.

Pets Teach Responsibility—to Parents

There are two kinds of parents in the world: those who've succumbed to their children's incessant pleading for a pet and those who are still putting up with it.

Maybe you're one of those parents who thought caring for a pet would teach responsibility. But after a few months with a new puppy, you're thinking, "Hey, wait! I already was responsible." The children who begged, pleaded and promised to walk the dog daily now have softball practice, summer camp and a case of amnesia. And instead of learning about responsibility, they're learning they can always count on you.

Or maybe, like me, you're looking for a way to teach your children about responsibility, give them the joy animals provide and stop the begging, all without actually getting a pet. This is a tall order, but I have three suggestions for you. And, speaking from experience, I can tell you that none of them work.

First, have plenty of friends and relatives who own pets your children can play with. If your friends and relatives don't have pets, give them some. You may be thinking that playing with other people's animals would only make your kids want their own pet more. And you would be right.

You may also be thinking that, if you give a friend a pet just so your children can play with it when you visit, you may not be invited to visit again. You would be right about that too. I told you these don't work.

Second, you can encourage your kids to pet sit. There are two kinds of pets a child will care for without being reminded: one that belongs to someone else who is paying them to take care of it and one they've owned for less than a month. You choose.

Pet sitting allows children to learn about responsibility without their parents having to learn any more about it. At least it works for some kids. My one and only pet sitting experience ended badly after an unfortunate incident with a beta. You're probably thinking, "How hard can it be to take care of a fish?" Well, that's what I thought too.

My son has been much more successful. He started his pet sitting career with some hermit crabs, graduated to a chinchilla and then "went to the dogs." And I had high hopes. I thought he'd change his mind about wanting a dog of his own after going to a friend's house several times a day, feeding and playing with her dogs, then waiting for them to "do their business." What an odd way to put it. Whoever came up with that term wasn't very pro-business. But I digress. The point is, business or no business, it didn't change Isaac's mind about wanting a pet.

Finally, you could compromise and get a small, low maintenance pet. A friend told me that if a child wants a dog, he or she would be wise to start by asking for a horse, then negotiating from there. My son made the mistake of asking for a dog first, so he got a hamster. And yes, I'm aware that many a family has started with a fish or bird and wound up with three rabbits, two cats and a St. Bernard to keep it company.

I think that's what my son is hoping for. He knows that I grew up with cats, dogs, rabbits, chickens and even a few pigs and sheep. And he knows I loved them all. I'm not sure how much they taught me about responsibility, but I did learn to count on my mother.

Three Goldfish, Two Hamsters and a Canary

My son was six when he asked me the question every parent dreads. Not *that* one. The other question every parent dreads. "Mom, can I have a dog?"

"Maybe someday," I hedged.

"How about a cat?"

"Maybe someday."

"What about a bird?"

"Maybe someday! Now good night!"

Moments passed. I thought he was asleep until he whispered, "Mommy?"

"Yes."

"Can you pet a fish?"

I was starting to think the child wanted a pet. His lobbying got worse after one of his cousins got a golden retriever puppy. Then an aunt got a Springer spaniel. The relatives weren't helping.

It's not that I don't like dogs. It's that I don't like work. To me, dogs are like Christmas lights; I love them at other people's homes. I'd love Christmas lights on my house too, but I don't want to climb up on the roof and put them there.

I know what you're saying. "You shouldn't put a dog on the roof anyway." Yes, I realize that. The point is, someone else does the work and I don't even have to remind them to do it.

I remained strong but Isaac started keeping all manner of bugs, worms and crawly things in shoeboxes in his bedroom. Somehow they always managed to escape mysteriously into the night, thanks to contacts they had on the outside. (Me.)

When I tried to kill a moth that had landed too high on our vaulted ceiling to reach, Isaac named it "Lonesome" and called out words of encouragement to it. "You're safe, Lonesome! She'll never get you up there!"

I was tempted to relent. Puppies are cuter than moths, plus they can help clean up under the dinner table. On the other hand, moths are quieter and they don't need shots.

To be fair, I had many pets while I was growing up and I loved them all. There was Buster the bulldog. Buster couldn't bark because of the surgery he'd had during his life with the carnival from which my father had rescued him. There was Laddie the collie, who was eventually given away because she started to bite the hand that fed her—as well as other body parts.

There were the cats: Tiny, who crawled into a dresser drawer and was accidentally imprisoned there for several days before my mother heard her pitiful mewing. And Froto, who ate the houseplants, including the cactus.

And there was my favorite pet of all: Bernie, part Chihuahua and part who-knew-what, who had a run-in with a car and lived to bark about it.

I suppose I learned something from all of them—not to chase cars or eat houseplants. I learned all about unconditional love from the dogs and unconditional contempt from the cats. But maybe the main lesson I learned was that my dear mother would never let an animal starve.

I was afraid my son would learn that too. Children can and do learn responsibility from having pets. But so do parents. No parent can stand by while a pet goes hungry. Plus homes start to smell funny when pets aren't cared for properly.

And that's exactly what I was worried about. Not that my house would smell funny; it already does. I was afraid that if we ever got a pet, my son wouldn't be the only one taking on new responsibilities. I would be too, and I wasn't handling the ones I had very well. No, if we were ever going to have a pet, it would have to be very low maintenance. I was leaning toward a Chia pet.

The next time my son asked if he could have a pet, which of course he did, I said, "Yes. Absolutely you can have a pet, when you're old enough to be responsible for it. Old enough to feed it and care for it. Old enough to know how it does and doesn't like to be held and petted. And," I added under my breath, "old enough to have a home of your own."

Lucky for Isaac, he didn't have to wait that long. And I blame the nice people who, because of their sincere love for children and blatant disregard for parents, give away free fish at children's events. I took my son to a school carnival, naively thinking the only danger would be cotton candy stuck to the car upholstery. But he soon discovered that if he tossed the ring onto the right bottle or caught a certain item with a plastic hook, he could win a fish. Actually, I think he could have won one just by saying, *"Me! Me!"* at the end of the evening when the carnival coordinator started begging people to take the fish.

At any rate, he left the carnival rejoicing, swinging a sandwich bag full of water and fish. And I left annoyed, praying the bag would stay closed during the drive home.

There are two things to remember about free fish. Number one, free fish are traumatized fish. They have endured long hours in small plastic bags with large faces—or rather small faces that look large to them—gawking like sharks just inches away. And they have suffered through the shaking of their little plastic homes by children who ache to cuddle and pet them, which most fish don't enjoy.

The second thing to remember about free fish is that they are not free. A fish can only live so long in a sandwich bag and as it turns out, only slightly longer in the $17 aquarium you buy to house it in. But I'm getting ahead of myself.

Along with the aquarium we bought some lovely blue rocks ($7.59) to make the aquarium more attractive for the fish, a net

($2.39) to gently move them when it was time to clean the aquarium (which my son promised to do often), fish food ($4.59) with omega-3 fatty acids and select vitamins to keep them healthy, and water conditioner ($2.99) to replace the natural slime coating they apparently need in times of stress—unlike the rest of us who find slime coating quite stressful.

Maybe there weren't quite enough omega-3 fatty acids in the food, because our first two free fish lasted only three days—one day for each omega. I know the water conditioner wasn't to blame, because the dead fish still looked plenty slimy to me.

After a suitable mourning period and a proper burial in the flowerbed, we washed the rocks and the aquarium and put the $35 worth of fish supplies in the closet. My son was thinking we'd keep it for the next free fish. I was thinking we'd keep it for the next garage sale.

Alas, a year went by. The annual carnival where we'd gotten the fish rolled around and again they were giving away fish. Amazingly, I resisted my son's pleas. I comforted him as best I could while silently congratulating myself on remaining fish free for another year.

And then there was another children's event just a few weeks later. And as luck would have it, they were giving away fish. My resistance had been lowered at the carnival, and after all, we did have $35 worth of fish provisions in our closet. We brought home free fish number three.

We decided to wait to name this one so that we wouldn't be too attached if it died, which it did three days later. Apparently three days is the life span of a free fish.

We were pet-free again, but children have an instinct for choosing the exact moment to ask for what they want. One day when I wasn't home, my son asked my husband, "If I keep my room clean for a month, can I please, please, *please* have a hamster?" And knowing him as I do, I'm sure he didn't just ask once. In my husband's defense, I have to say he was distracted at the moment. Besides he was in a weakened state, having already said no to a dog, a cat, a rabbit and a bird. Mostly, in his wildest dreams, he never thought it would happen.

But dang if it didn't. And suddenly, as my son put it so eloquently, we finally had a pet with hair: Monsieur Hamstie Doodle Pie Rosby.

A hamster isn't bad as pets go. Hamstie didn't purr when we petted him or come running to greet us when we came home after a long day at work. There was very little tail to wag. But he didn't shed either. Or beg for table scraps. Or bite the mailman.

And he didn't cost much. The cage was a hand-me-down from another set of parents who I'm sure were happy to be out of the hamster business.

Monsieur Hamstie didn't need to be taken out for a walk. He was quiet other than the constant whir of the hamster wheel. And if we could have figured out how to hook up the wheel to a generator, we would have saved enough on electricity to pay for his food and bedding.

He was a good eater. He liked nuts, fruit and whole wheat bread, and he loved cruciferous vegetables. In fact, thanks to Monsieur Hamstie, we all ate more of them. He certainly couldn't eat a head of cabbage by himself.

And hamsters are apparently hardier than free goldfish are. We had Hamstie for a couple of years before he went to that Great Hamster Wheel in the Sky. He was replaced quickly by Bo-Bo, and I'd almost say it was worth the trouble, except that having a hamster did not keep my son from asking for a dog.

Long after the fish and both our hamsters had died, we compromised again. Some friends were giving away a canary and my son wanted it desperately, even though it's no larger than a hamster and it doesn't have hair. I finally agreed because the pleading was relentless and also because it was still not a dog.

Mr. Tweeters didn't warm to us right away. I was concerned he might be unhappy about his cage. As I'm sure you know, birds are uniquely designed to fly, but the cage he came in was approximately the size of two shoe boxes put together—if your feet are big. So we bought him a bigger, more expensive cage, proving once again that there is no such thing as a free pet. It's beautiful, a mansion of a cage, if your mansion has bars for walls and water troughs instead of faucets.

And it's worth it. Mr. Tweeters seems much happier; at least he's singing to us more. Well maybe not to us. According to my research, he's probably singing to claim his territory and attract a girlfriend. He can have the territory, but there will be no girlfriend, not if I have my way. But then I don't always get my way. Witness the fact that we've had three goldfish, two hamsters and a canary. On the other hand, we've still never had a dog.

Break Bread over Their Heads

Mexican children eat Mexican food. Japanese children eat Japanese food. Australian children eat Australian food. They don't eat it because of genetics. They eat it because their parents eat it. They eat it because they're hungry and it's there.

This sums up my philosophy for convincing children to eat a variety of healthful foods: serve them. And it has led me to put an assortment of not particularly kid-friendly foods on the table in the hopes that Isaac will learn to eat them. Sometimes it works. He has been known to eat grapefruit, avocados, Brussels sprouts and broccoli. Of course, he has also been known not to eat them.

But the most difficult part of putting my philosophy into practice is having other kids join us for meals. I know their parents cook nutritious foods—just different nutritious foods. Maybe better tasting too. And I'm starting to worry that my son will grow up with healthy eating habits but no friends.

One night we invited "Scott" to stay for dinner. Having experienced dinner at our house, Scott knew enough to ask what we were having before he agreed to stay. He seemed relieved, even pleased, when I told him we were having steak. I didn't tell him it was Swiss steak. Moments later as he sat down to dinner, Scott looked downright betrayed. "I wonder what my mom is cooking for dinner."

Spinach-mashed potatoes happened to be on the menu the evening "Brian" was over. Low-fat creamed spinach mashed into potatoes is one of my son's favorites—really. We have two mealtime rules at our house: try everything and keep your mouth shut, and not just while you chew. If you like it, you're free to talk about it all you want. But our normally well-mannered guest was so stunned by the green heap on his plate that he couldn't help himself. He compared the potatoes to something I cannot say in print. He went home hungry and I vowed to serve guacamole the next time he comes over—if he ever does.

"Michael" was polite but cautious as he tasted my split pea soup. He took tiny bites and chewed them as long as you'd chew a piece of bubble gum. (This isn't normally necessary with split pea soup—not even mine.) But at least he was eating—until the ladybug found its way from the great outdoors to the middle of his whole-wheat toast. Michael's eyes widened, his spoon clattered to the table, and he ate no more. The ladybug never did try the soup—as far as we know.

One evening I succumbed to macaroni (whole wheat) and cheese for my son and his overnight guest, "Tim." But I topped it off with homemade chicken strips—white meat coated in wheat germ. Tim was polite, but, oddly enough, not very hungry. The next day when he joined us for lunch, I served the remainder of the chicken. He sat down at the table, raised his eyebrows, and said, "Do you always eat your leftovers?"

I'm sure he told his parents about lunch later while foraging through their refrigerator. My son tells me what he eats at other people's homes, and it's almost always better. He went on and on once about the cold cut sandwiches he'd had at "Brian's" house. They were made with white bread—a delicacy.

I know what you're thinking; the food might not be the problem. It may be the skill of the chef that led to the above incidents. And you may be right. I once served spaghetti to my son and his buddy "David." I didn't feel good about this. For one thing, it was leftover spaghetti. And while the sauce was the kid-friendly canned variety, it was supplemented with extra green peppers, onions and mushrooms. But I'm thrifty—and lazy—so that's what we were having for lunch. Unbelievably, our seven-year-old guest ate three helpings and then said five little words that endeared him to me forever: "Can I have your recipe?"

Wouldn't you know it? My husband had made the spaghetti.

Winning the Birthday Party Competition

If you ask me, children's birthday parties have gotten out of hand. I don't even recall having a birthday party when I was a child, let alone renting a swimming pool for one. But we didn't have a swimming pool to rent in my hometown. We had a lake. And you didn't have to rent it, but you did have to chase the cows off the beach.

Also, my mother was a busy woman. There were ten children in my family. One does not plan ten birthday parties per year unless one is a professional party planner.

Of course, I did attend birthday parties as a child. And I was once hurt deeply when, as I handed my gift to the birthday girl, she said with feeling, "I hope it's not another paint-by-number." I grew up in a very small town. The local hardware and drug stores had the only toy departments in town and I happen to know they both had fine selections of paint-by-number sets.

I was invited to a few other parties as a child, but far fewer than my son has attended in his short life. (Maybe because I had a reputation for giving paint-by-number sets.) Isaac has been to parties at arcades, hotels and fast food restaurants. He's been to swimming parties, skating parties, paintball parties and even a disco party. As

-63-

a result, he always expects his mother to come up with something equally exciting. Poor thing; he has the wrong mother.

My birthday party-deprived childhood left me completely unprepared to plan birthday parties that can compete with the modern variety. I've never even made what you could call a real birthday cake and I see no reason to start now. That's why there are bakeries. I did put five candles in the peanut butter sandwich I made for Isaac's fifth birthday breakfast. He loves peanut butter sandwiches. And I don't make waffles either.

It doesn't mean I love him less. Here's what I tell people who make their children cakes in the shape of cartoon characters or choo-choo trains: "After work every day, I have just a few hours to spend with my son. I could spend that time making a birthday cake in the shape of a train, or I could get down on my hands and knees and actually play train with him. I choose the latter." I don't mention that I couldn't make a train cake if I tried.

Unfortunately, homemade theme cakes and matching party paraphernalia are an important part of birthday parties for the elementary school set. While I distributed store-bought birthday cake at one of my lackluster parties, a young guest told me that his mother actually makes his birthday cakes. I told him I love my son too much to do that to him.

The child persisted. "Usually," he said, "homemade tastes better."

I said, "That depends on whose home it was made in. Now eat your cake or I will."

Along with my lack of experience, birthday party horror stories add to my anxiety. At a birthday party thrown by some friends, a blindfolded guest missed the piñata and whacked another partygoer. A friend's daughter broke her arm at a birthday party. And a little boy brought unwanted guests to one of my nephew's parties: head lice.

Another issue for me is the gifts. Ten guests equal ten gifts and, while I'm sure he would disagree, I think my son needs more toys like I need more dirty dishes in my sink.

And then there's that small matter of being responsible for other people's children when I'm not sure I'm qualified to care for my own.

But above all, I'm intimidated by stories of sensational children's parties, where the parents rent a limousine, hire a celebrity entertainer or take all the guests to Disneyland. My idea of a good party is plenty of guacamole, which many children don't seem to appreciate.

How can I compete? I can't. Nevertheless I've managed some semblance of a birthday party every year since my son was old enough to care. Here's how I did it:

The Fast Food Restaurant Option

On the advice of a friend, I called a fast food restaurant to plan Isaac's fifth birthday party. I was ecstatic to learn that the restaurant would provide not only kids meals but a birthday cake as well. Their play area would provide the entertainment for the kids. That left me responsible only for sending invitations and picking out the birthday gift—or using the toy in the kid's meal, which I'm ashamed to admit I actually considered.

Sounded easy enough but it was exhausting. Being in charge of eight five-year-olds is like supervising a roomful of grasshoppers. Still, it was a success by my criteria: no body parts were broken. Nobody wanted his gift back. And nobody wanted his mother before the party was over. At least no one mentioned it if he did, and members of this particular demographic group are not known for keeping their thoughts to themselves.

Even the birthday cake was a hit. It may not have looked like a choo-choo train or a cartoon character, but it was decorated magnificently…with the logo of a certain popular fast food restaurant.

The Rent-An-Activity Option

Another year I booked the party at a bowling alley. I did have some concerns—many small feet and many large bowling balls in the same room, to name one. But what could be more fun for a group of first graders than dropping large balls onto a shiny, hardwood floor?

This party might have been a success except for one thing. Four parents who had not bothered to RSVP brought their kids anyway—and then left. Suddenly we had nine children but only one bowling lane. This did allow the kids plenty of time for activities between bowling. Unfortunately, we hadn't planned any.

The Sleepover Option

A sleepover is one of the least expensive children's birthday parties you can have—unless you count pain and suffering. And thus far this has been my son's favorite kind of party. I do not share his enthusiasm. For reasons I don't recall from my own childhood, when you're young it's a luxury to stay up late and feel miserable the next day.

Everyone knows a sleepover is not a sleepover. It could more accurately be called a layover, a brief layover. The only ones sleeping during a sleepover are the parents of the guests—not that they don't deserve it.

Even knowing the truth, many parents, beaten down by their child's pleading, consent to sleepovers. If you find yourself in this situation, I have some tips to help your party stand up to the competition.

First of all, keep it small. At his most recent sleepover, my son had four boys stay the night. This is a good number. Still, for some reason it seemed like many more.

Remain calm. It can be upsetting to have a child who is not your own run into your house screaming, "I am bleeding to death!" It's upsetting to hear your own child scream that too, but you're better able to interpret his or her cries for the theatrics they are.

Use the television for the purpose for which it was intended: sedation. I'm not generally a fan of television, but a child's sleepover party is one time when it can be useful. Television is the opiate of the elementary school masses and it is a legal opiate. Use it.

Don't bother picking up until your guests have all gone home. Certainly nag the children to pick up after themselves but do it from your place on the couch. Picking up in a house full of children is like shoveling snow during a blizzard or drying off while you're still in the shower.

Play games at bedtime, but not board games, head games. Tell the children that certainly they may wake up as early as they wish, but if they are the first to wake up, they must lie perfectly still with their eyes closed tightly until everyone else is awake. Hopefully it will be at least 6 a.m. before they begin to wonder how they will know that everyone else is awake if they are all lying perfectly still with their eyes closed.

Finally, remember that, unlike other parties, a sleepover is not over when the guests go home. Plan on devoting a great deal of time and energy to putting your home back in order. Be prepared to spend the next few weeks returning miscellaneous items such as toys, sleeping bags, jackets and dirty socks to their owners. Expect the birthday person to be cranky, disagreeable and not the least bit appreciative in the days following the sleepover. And finally, count on him or her to ask for another one next year.

If This Is so Fun, Why Is Everyone Screaming?

An amusement park is, by definition, many people standing in line, waiting their turn to become nauseated and paying a lot of money for the privilege. Against my better judgment I have agreed to accompany my six-year old son to the spine-tingling, hair-raising world that is Snoopy Land, the amusement park at the Mall of America.

I'm not worried though. I've invited our 16-year-old Japanese exchange student to come along. Yukari, being young and adventurous, will go on the rides with Isaac and save me the trouble. I'll pay for their fun and look very generous while I relax on a bench and eat snow cones. It will be grand. That's my plan anyway.

Then Yukari informs me that while she's willing to try some rides, she doesn't really like that sort of thing. It's clear she's assuming I'll ride with Isaac. Uh-oh. I guess I didn't make it clear why I brought her along.

Isaac gets excited riding the glass elevator on our way to Snoopy Land. In a last ditch effort to save myself, I say, "Hey, we can ride this as much as we want—and it's *free*." He thinks I'm kidding.

Moments later we're standing in line and I'm listening to the screaming and watching in horror as people are tossed willy-nilly by one machine or another. And I realize it goes against every instinct in me to fall from high places or spin out of control. People who enjoy roller coasters, bungee jumping and the like clearly have underdeveloped survival instincts and should be closely supervised. My son falls into this category—no pun intended. And apparently I'm the one who's going to have to supervise him.

Right off he wants to try a ride that turns an entire audience upside down and swings them around like a toy in the hands of a toddler. I try to reason with him. "If it's so fun, why is everyone screaming?"

I feel queasy just watching. I get the same effect if I ride too long in the back seat of a moving car. I see no reason to pay for it.

Thankfully Isaac doesn't quite measure up to the height mark, the line that one must surpass in order to get on the ride. "Aw, that's too bad," I say, feeling hopeful. Maybe there'll be others he can't ride. Then we discover he's plenty tall for the roller coaster. And he squeals with excitement for the duration.

I weep.

At the bottom we're offered the opportunity to buy a candid snap shot of our adventure in return for the rest of our vacation money. My son looks like he just saw Santa Claus. I look like I just saw something unrecognizable on my dinner plate. I don't buy the photo.

Next we head for the Log Chute, an "unforgettable four-minute, water-borne expedition, traveling up, around and through a 70-foot mountain," or so the promotional material says.

Log riders survive (one hopes) two dramatic plunges, the last one being forty feet down, directly into a lake. It's hard for me to muster much enthusiasm; I had whiplash once, and it wasn't that great.

Then Yukari points out quite accurately, but too late for us to change our minds, that our logs don't have seat belts. I put on my seat belt every time I get in a car, and I've never plunged even close to forty feet while driving. Isaac tells us that if we crash on the log chute we're probably better off falling out. Neither one of us is reassured.

We're at the top of the last forty-foot drop and Yukari says with feeling, "I don't want to do this!" I don't either, but at this point, I don't see many options. I wonder if my insurance is up to date.

We survive the plunges and the roller coaster and an assortment of other costly contraptions. My son skips off the last one. I stagger off—wet, wobbly and broke. My head hurts. I have a stomachache and I feel like lying down.

He wants a chili dog and curly fries.

III
Keeping Your Kids Enthused about School and You Enthused about Them

Walking Backwards to Kindergarten

It was more than forty years ago, but I still recall vividly the trauma of my first day of kindergarten. A fellow student asked me if I was a boy or a girl. I still have psychological scars from the incident, which was made even more painful by the fact that I was wearing a new pink dress.

That remains my most vivid memory of kindergarten, but one I chose not to share with Isaac as he was preparing to start kindergarten. I did tell him about my teacher, a kind, grandmotherly women who taught kindergarten in her living room. I told him how wonderful the snacks were and that even after all these years, I still miss naptime. None of these seemed to pique his interest.

I told him that my teacher had awesome toys, all of which she allowed her students to play with. And I told him about my favorite, a pink crocheted doll that wasn't a toy at all; it sat on a roll of toilet paper in my teacher's bathroom. This didn't make kindergarten any more attractive to my son either.

Other than those and the ABC song, I had very few memories of kindergarten to share with him. And he already knew the ABC song.

Today's children do know a lot more than I did when I started kindergarten. They already know their colors, shapes and numbers.

They can write their names and recite their addresses and phone numbers. And they know much more about dinosaurs than those of us who were born closer to the time dinosaurs roamed the earth.

But despite their knowledge, they're still as apprehensive about starting school as we were. I realize some parents pressure their children by telling them success in kindergarten will determine which colleges they get into, how well they'll do in their careers and how soon they'll be able to retire from them. But I wasn't aware of putting such pressure on my son. Still at one point he said, "I wish you'd never signed me up for kindergarten."

When children are anxious, their parents are anxious too. To help ease both our minds, we went to the local library and checked out storybooks on the subject of kindergarten. This wasn't very reassuring though, since the children in the books could count backward from 100, speak a second language and name all the presidents in order, none of which I can do.

We let him choose his new school clothes and select his supplies, including a new Rocket Power backpack. His teacher sent him a letter welcoming him into her class. He said, "I bet she says that to all the kids."

Still when the big day arrived, he did seem somewhat excited. He picked out his clothes carefully, a favorite T-shirt and a new pair of pants. I took him to lunch at one of his favorite restaurants. Later we walked towards the school hand in hand.

From the time our children are born, they begin to walk away from us. Some of their steps are just so much bigger than others. The ones Isaac was taking at that moment seemed that way to me. I felt like crying.

He interrupted my reverie to inform me that we were going the long way. He knew exactly where his classroom was. He took his hand from mine and walked on ahead, a little man. Oh my.

Then I saw something that reassured me he'd still need his mother for a while. The new pants he'd chosen so carefully for his first day of kindergarten were on backwards.

Keep Your Kids Enthused about School and You Enthused about Your Kids

Any excitement children feel about being back in school disappears as fast as your budget for their school clothing did. This school year was less than a week old when Isaac told me he wished it were over.

But it isn't just school itself that loses its shine. Children are so excited about their school clothes, for example, that they'd wear them to bed if we'd let them. Two weeks after school starts, the new clothes join the old ones in a heap on the bedroom floor.

We had a dress code when I was in elementary school—a "dress" dress code. Girls were required to wear dresses no matter what the weather. The boys also had a dress code—but it wasn't quite as inconvenient. They had to wear belts—and pants. They were not allowed to wear dresses.

At the beginning of each school year, I didn't mind the dress code. I had many beautiful dresses that my grandmother had sewn for me, and I was always excited to wear them for the first time. Unfortunately, a "dress" dress code can be a hardship for a little girl who likes to play at recess as much as her male counterparts do. Scabbed knees detract from the look of a pretty little dress. And, I happen to know, climbing a chain link fence can destroy it entirely.

The newness wears off accessories too. In fourth grade, I was actually excited when the principal called my parents to tell them I needed glasses. I thought glasses were fashionable—until I had to wear them. Still I swear it wasn't vanity when I broke my new glasses playing tetherball. It was a lack of athletic ability.

There is even a time—a very short time—in their school careers when some children think homework sounds exciting. This time is, of course, before they actually have to do it. On his first day of first grade a few years back, my son did his small amount of "homework" in the car on the way home from school. I had a feeling his enthusiasm wouldn't last. It didn't. Not even until the second day.

I can't blame him. It didn't last for me either. Miss Weiland, who was one of my favorite teachers even after the incident I'm about to describe, actually asked my class if we *wanted* to start having homework for the first time in sixth grade. The very idea of her giving us a choice in the matter sounds ludicrous now, but Miss Weiland knew what she was doing. If my memory serves me correctly (which is unlikely), she asked us to lay our heads on our desks, close our eyes and then raise our hands if we wanted homework. Unbelievable as it sounds, I do not remember how I voted. I'm sure the "work" part of homework disturbed me, just as it would today. On the other hand, I recall desperately wanting to be more like the big kids, i.e. the seventh and eighth graders. I must not have been alone; my sixth grade class voted in homework.

Today I can't help but wonder: was my class more academically ambitious than we appeared to be during the rest of our educational career? Did the rest of the class want to look more grown up too? Or did dear Miss Weiland, whom we loved and trusted, rig the vote without sacrificing any of her popularity? Whatever the case, it was a clever strategy on her part. When we lost our enthusiasm for homework after one take-home math assignment, we had only ourselves to blame.

These days there is no choice about it; children will have homework and as parents we may feel the need to ride herd on them until they get it done. This can be a great anxiety producer—for the children too. While the following tips won't ensure that your children maintain their enthusiasm for homework, they may help you maintain your enthusiasm for your children.

1. First and foremost, while you may support your child as he or she does homework, you must never do the homework yourself. I have no trouble following this rule, because I understand less and less of Isaac's work. I've learned to leave the room when I check his homework so I can use the dictionary and the calculator without him seeing.

2. Create a space dedicated to homework. It should be quiet, comfortable and well lit. If it's in the home of a fine tutor, so much the better.

3. Remain calm. It may seem like a good idea at the time, but one sure way to squelch learning is to tear a worksheet out of your child's hands and scream, "*Just let me do it*" Instead try asking gentle, probing questions. "Is there another way to look at that?" "Did you check your work?" "Whatever made me think I could be a parent?"

4. Most importantly, be ready to handle with authority the three most common comments children make while doing homework:

   A. We don't do it that way.

   Responding correctly to this comment is a challenge because, number one, they may do it differently these days. Number two, and more likely, you may be doing it wrong. And what's more, you may have always done it wrong. When in doubt, feel free to ask the child's teacher for an explanation. There is no reason to be embarrassed to admit that you don't understand her second grade homework.

   B. Why do I need to learn this?

   Appeal to your child's higher instincts with something like, "Because you must do well in school so that you can get into a good college, so that you can get a high-paying job, so that you can reimburse me for college expenses and support me in my old age at the level to which I've become accustomed and possibly higher." If this isn't effective, and it may not be, say, "So that someday, you can win a truck load of money on *Jeopardy*."

C. Could I watch TV first?
Try, "No, but you could clean your room first."

Attack of the Backpack

I used to lecture Isaac about how hard I had it back when I had to walk miles and miles uphill both ways to school. Then I tried lifting his backpack.

Soon he'll join the masses of students happily packing up all their new school supplies. They won't be this excited again until next spring when they dump their backpacks out all over their bedroom floors. And who can blame them? Studies estimate that many students carry loads heavier than 15 percent of their body weight. That's the limit recommended by the American Academy of Orthopedic Surgeons, who's apparently been boning up on the subject. (I carry a purse that's heavier than 15 percent of my body weight too, but that's a topic for another day.)

On my way to work, I regularly see kids with giant packs, looking like turtles walking upright. I worry they're going to tip over backwards and be pinned to the ground, their little arms and legs flailing while they try to get up. Late for school again!

Back when you and I were in school, we didn't have as many extracurricular activities, at least not activities requiring all the accompanying clothing and equipment. We didn't have all those electronic devices. And Crayola wasn't making as many colors yet.

But the biggest contributor to the backpack burden is textbooks, which should not be left at school all year long, no matter what your kids tell you. There are more textbooks now, and they're heavier. A lot has happened since we were young, so history books have had to expand. And long ago, there were just the three Rs: readin', 'ritin' and 'rithmatic. Eventually there were more courses added to the curriculum. Luckily, one of them was spelling.

What can be done to protect our kids from the attack of the backpack? First take care to choose the right model and size. A good rule of thumb is never to buy a backpack that's larger than your child.

You might even consider a wheeled backpack. If your child doesn't think those are cool enough, you could get them a wheelbarrow. Those are plenty cool, though they don't maneuver well on stairs.

Occasionally you should supervise when your kids are packing their backpacks. Children sometimes get confused about what is and what is not essential at school. Pencils are essential; a Nintendo Game Boy II is not. Paper is essential; a Super Soaker Scatter Blaster squirt gun is not. There's no sense in loading a backpack full of items that the teacher will just confiscate later.

Finally, backpacks should be carried over both shoulders to distribute the weight evenly. This will keep your child from looking like a middle-aged woman who's been carrying a purse the size of a suitcase over the same shoulder since she was a teenager. No child I know wants to look like a middle-aged woman, even the ones who will be middle-aged women someday.

Having said all of that, I have to add that carrying a backpack is only part of the problem. In my extensive internet research I came across a study of backpack injuries. Only thirteen percent of the backpack injuries reported in this particular study were caused by wearing one. Another thirteen percent were caused by being *hit* by one, and as much as those things weigh, you can see why that would hurt. I'm surprised there were no fatalities.

Amazingly twenty-eight percent of backpack injuries were actually caused by tripping over them. This confirms what I've been telling Isaac for years: leaving a backpack unopened in the middle of the living room floor all weekend could be hazardous to his health.

How Long Will it Take Dorothy to Do 22 Math Problems?

If you tell yourself you're bad at something, it becomes a self-fulfilling prophecy. That's why when my son asks for help with his math homework, I never say, "I'm no good at math." I say, "Go ask your father."

My husband is a former elementary school teacher whom I once caught thumbing through an old calculus book for fun. I never took calculus and I remember nothing of algebra or geometry. I take that back. I do know a rectangle when I see one. But I'm a journalism major with an English minor who didn't realize until recently that telling myself I'm no good at math would make it so. (Oh, and if you catch any grammar errors in this essay, remember it's an English minor, not an English major.)

Thankfully it takes all kinds; it just takes some kinds longer to do math. And at my house, that's the kind that's usually around at homework time. As a liberal arts person, I have to say my least favorite of all math problems are story problems. Story problems take something I'm very fond of—stories—and turn them into something I'm not fond of at all: math problems.

I realize story problems are real life problems and that we encounter them on a daily basis. Take this example: Dorothy is baking a chocolate cake. The recipe calls for ... oh wait. Bad

-81-

example. I never bake cake, though I do eat cake, sometimes multiple pieces.

But let's try another example: Mrs. Rosby's son Isaac needs $250 for the camp he's attending this summer. He also needs a new pair of shoes, which will cost anywhere from $20 to $50 depending on what kind of mood Mrs. Rosby is in the day they go shopping. Mrs. Rosby has $17. How much money will Mrs. Rosby need to win on scratch lottery tickets in order to pay her son's expenses? And how many years until he can get a job so he can pay them himself? (Oh, and don't call me Mrs. Rosby. It makes me sound old. How many years older does it make me sound?)

When I help my son with story problems, the liberal arts major in me can't help but come out, as you'll see from the following story problems taken from actual math worksheets.

Problem 1: Each week Sarah washes dishes three nights, washes clothes one night, empties trash cans two nights, and cooks supper one night. If you stop by randomly one evening, what are the chances that Sarah would be cooking dinner? A math person would say "one in seven." (I think.) I say, "What are the chances that Sarah could come to my house a few nights a week?" (I like stories with happy endings.)

Problem 2: David can walk 12 blocks in five minutes. If each block is 50 feet long, how many feet will David walk during the 30 minutes he walks his dog? A math person would say 3600 feet—or something like that. I say, "That depends. Does the dog have to pee?"

Problem 3: Dorothy has 22 math problems to do. She completes one problem every three minutes. In hours and minutes, how long will it take Dorothy to complete all 22 problems? A math person would say, "One hour and six minutes." I say, "One problem every *three minutes*? Are you joking? That's no self-fulfilling prophecy; that's a miracle."

Snowstorms Not What They Used to Be

There is no announcement that will make your children happier than, "Go back to bed, school is called off." Except maybe, "We're getting a puppy." It usually has to be a whopper of a winter storm to bring on the school-closing announcement, but that doesn't stop children from hoping for it August through May.

At least it doesn't stop Isaac. We've had snow this winter, but no school closings. Still, every time he sees snow falling, he asks. Every time he sees a snowflake, he asks. Every time he sees his mittens, he asks if school will be called off.

I was no different when I was a child. I loved snow days. With ten children in the house, my parents may not have found them so pleasant. Nor do I anymore. Snowstorms just aren't what they used to be.

When I was a child, my father plowed the streets in our little town. He always started in front of our house since the equipment was stored nearby. So, by the time I was out of bed, there were gargantuan snow piles all around our parking area ready for me to climb. But the road outside my present home isn't the first one plowed. When the snowplow finally does come, it still leaves a large pile of snow perfect for climbing, but it leaves it on the entrance to my driveway.

They still call off school, but no one ever calls off work. And there is something disconcerting about listening to a radio announcer repeat, "No travel advised," while one is driving to the babysitter's through a blinding snowstorm.

I think my childhood love for snow was dealt its final blow the day I had to park at the bottom of my large hill and carry a toddler and two bags of groceries up it through knee deep snow.

But children, including the one I once carried up the hill, play in the snow. They roll in it and sled on it. They make snow angels and snowmen. Children frolic in snow. Adults shovel it.

Grown-ups shiver in the cold. At least this one does. Kids pile their coats at the top of the hill and sled down in their wet sweatshirts. We buy them hats and mittens and warm coats. They lose their hats and mittens and warm coats and don't find them again until they no longer fit.

Snowstorms fill children with the urge to make snowmen. Snowstorms fill mothers with the urge to make cookies and other hot, hardy comfort food. Children take three bites and run out into the snow. Parents eat the rest then plop down on the couch to watch the Weather Channel.

When we were kids, we dreamed of snowstorms and school being called off. As adults, we dream of spring. When we were kids we headed to the ski slopes and the sledding hills. As adults, we head to Arizona. Well … I don't, but I want to.

No, snowstorms just aren't what they used to be. I realize there are adults who love snow. They ski, they snowmobile, they snowshoe. And I expect I'll enjoy snow more myself, and my son will like it less, when he's old enough to shovel it.

Wiggling Your Way to Spiritual Growth

Against my better judgment, I agreed to teach Sunday school for several years. I peeled rambunctious students off the ceiling. I helped those having trouble with their art projects—lucky for me these were second and third grade art projects. And I handled a variety of important requests, the main one being, "Can I go to the bathroom?"

I'm not sure I actually taught the children anything. Teaching Sunday school is harder than it sounds. A room full of second graders is a lot like a working popcorn popper with the lid off. And my only on-the-job training was accidental. Once the previous year I had found myself in charge of a group of first graders when their teacher was running late. It didn't go well.

I stood guard while we waited, and to pass the time I suggested we draw on the blackboard. By some secret form of communication that I wasn't privy to, one of the children convinced the others to draw—how can I say this discreetly—derrieres on the blackboard. And I didn't tell the kids this, but they weren't half bad.

I'm proud to say my son was not the instigator. I'm not proud to say he was an enthusiastic participant.

As I scrambled for an eraser I couldn't help but wonder how I would explain this "artwork" to the regular Sunday school teacher if she happened to walk in at that moment.

After that episode I should have had the good sense to say no to teaching Sunday school myself, but alas, the following year I found myself in charge of a class of second graders.

While the children may have grown wiser in the interim, I apparently had not. I was stumped when a little girl asked me, "Is Osama Bin Laden part of God's family?"

I mumbled what must be the understatement of the century: "He made some bad choices, didn't he?"

On another occasion, we were discussing what new things God was doing in the children's lives. One little girl said she had something new in her life and asked me to guess what it was? "You have a new baby brother," I said confidently.

"He's three months old. That's not new."

"What is new in your life then?"

"I tasted dog food."

She seemed offended when I pointed out that God probably didn't have anything to do with that.

While I may not have taught my students much during my stint as a Sunday school teacher, I did learn a few things. I learned not only the words, but the gestures to "When I Wiggle, When I Giggle." And I learned again just how much second graders do wiggle and giggle.

I discovered that bribery is the best way to control a room full of children. Everyone who is sitting quietly gets a cookie. And I learned that after the cookies are eaten there is no more recourse.

And I learned that second graders need to go to the bathroom more than any other demographic group, including pregnant women.

Give Children Chores So You Don't Have to Do Them

As parents, we believe it's important for our children to do chores, mainly because we don't want to do them ourselves. Unfortunately, at this busy time in our lives when we could really use the help, we're sometimes hesitant to ask for it. For one thing, it's almost always faster and more efficient to do things ourselves. Your kids load the dishwasher and when you unload it later you find two broken glasses and a couple of really clean chicken bones. When my son washes dishes, we need to mop the floor too. Who has time for both?

And asking for help from children invariably leads to a fight or a demand for payment. Plus, the busier our lives are the less vital we consider some chores to be. It's hard to tell my son to clean his room when he's seen what mine looks like.

And finally, teaching the skills necessary to complete certain chores takes time we (and they) don't always have. When my son is busy with homework and extracurricular activities, I can't teach him to cook. (I probably couldn't anyway.)

But during the summer, when kids have no homework and fewer activities, there's nothing like a list of chores to stop them from complaining about boredom. And chores are an investment in their future—and ours. The inconvenience of assigning them now is much less than the inconvenience of having unemployed offspring living with us for the rest of our days.

And it can be fun. When Isaac helps me sort laundry we shoot baskets with the dirty clothes. We toss the whites across the room into one laundry basket for five points and the towels into another for ten points. I always let him win. I can get him to do practically all of it that way.

Teaching responsibility through household tasks starts early and lasts until the child moves out, stays out and stops asking for money.

Even children as young as two and three can begin taking on responsibility. They can brush their teeth, though you have to keep them from eating the toothpaste. They can also help select their own clothing for the day. You might be horrified at what they choose, but horror at what your children wear is going to be a fact of life for the next 20 years, just as it was for your parents. You may as well start getting used to it.

Between the ages four and five, children can help set the table, though you might want to take care of the glasses and the steak knives yourself. They can help empty small trashcans too, but if they see anything of theirs in the trash, it's probably coming back out.

Between the ages of six and eight, children can rake leaves, though you should allow plenty of time for tossing, rolling and re-raking. And they can start setting their own alarm clock—though for some, actually getting out of bed on their own may not be possible until they're adults.

Children ages nine to eleven can load the dishwasher on their own. But if you delegate this chore too early, you'll have nothing left but Tupperware. By this age they should also be able to fold their clothes and put them away. I attempted this too early. Once when his newly folded clothes looked more like a heap than a stack, I asked Isaac if he was folding his shirts the way I'd showed him to. He said, "Mine are like snowflakes. Every one is different." Lovely. Unfortunately, when every one is different, the drawer doesn't close.

By ages twelve to fourteen, children should be able to wash their own clothes, though you might not want them washing yours yet. They could also begin caring for younger siblings, much to the dismay of the younger siblings.

Finally, parenting experts point out that chores are just one of the ways children learn responsibility. They also learn it in school and in extracurricular activities, as well as by positive role modeling. But I can't really speak to that.

Fine Line between a Home-Cooked Meal and a Kitchen Fire

One Saturday morning I came home from exercising, and was greeted by the smell of smoke as I walked in the door. The aloe vera plant, which we use for burn first aid, was sitting on the banister. It could mean only one thing: breakfast!

Another mother might have panicked, but not me. There were no flames, there was laughter coming from the kitchen and most importantly, there was the smell of frying bacon. I couldn't make a fuss; I might not get any.

Sure enough Isaac and his friend were cooking. Every dish in the kitchen was dirty and every cupboard door was wide open. What could I do? I asked if there was enough for me. And there was. There was also enough for the boys' aunts, uncles and cousins as well as the neighbors down the street—none of whom were there to enjoy it.

I don't mean to brag, but it was fabulous—and I'm not just saying that because I didn't have to cook it. Along with bacon and toast, there was a very creative fried potato dish containing sautéed mushrooms, carrots, celery, onions, pepperoni, a variety of spices and even chopped walnuts. It really was delicious. Unfortunately, it can never be duplicated because of its complexity.

I had to resist the urge to ask the boys if they'd washed the mushrooms—and their hands. It was too late for that and I didn't want to squelch their youthful enthusiasm. My goal is to raise a child who cooks so that I don't have to.

When it comes to raising children who cook, naturally the first priority is safety. The basic rules are:

1. Cleanliness is vital. Give your guests food poisoning once, and they'll never be back.
2. If it can cut meat, it can cut you.
3. There is a fine line between a home-cooked meal and a kitchen fire. The faint smell of smoke in the air provided me with the perfect opportunity to tell the boys calmly about the smoke point of oil. Then I told them about the flash point of oil, only not as calmly.

The second priority is taste. The basic rules are:

1. A little goes a long way. Once you've dumped in half a can of cinnamon, it's hard to take it back out.
2. You can work around a lot of mistakes in the kitchen, but you can't uncook something once it's been overcooked.
3. Variety is nice. That's why there are so many flavors of Ranch dressing and Ramen noodles.

That pretty much covers everything I know about cooking. But in the area of child psychology, I can add a few things.

Parents should never squelch creativity by saying, "Nobody puts walnuts in fried potatoes." The mother of the first chef who put cheese on a hamburger or butter on crab legs didn't say, "Nobody does that." And if she did she's sorry now.

And parents must encourage their young chefs by eating what they cook. Or at least tasting what they cook. Or at least pretending to taste what they cook. This becomes a lot easier when your children quit cooking with Play-Doh and start cooking with bacon.

Give Kids an Allowance So You Can Borrow from Them Later

Sometimes it seems like children think money grows on trees. But today's children really are smarter than that; they know very well it shoots out of ATM machines. One of the best ways to teach them it's limited is to give them an allowance. An allowance helps them begin to realize they must make hard choices among the many things they want—or they must ask Grandpa.

It teaches them how money grows when they save it and how it disappears forever when they spend it—unless they kept the receipt and didn't break the Darth Vader voice changer they now want to return.

But there are advantages for parents too, and not just that we can borrow from our kids without a credit check. For one thing, we can ask them to start paying for some of the items we normally pay for: for example, movie tickets, snacks and dental check-ups.

And an allowance provides us with ready answers to some of our children's most annoying questions. When they say, "All the kids have it, why can't I?" we can say, "Because you don't have enough money." And when they say, "Can I have the $100 sneakers?" we can say, "Absolutely—when you have $100."

Most importantly, we hope an allowance will help us raise fiscally responsible children who won't default on any loans we cosign for them or raid our retirement fund to pay their gambling debts.

I've been doling out a weekly allowance since my son was six or seven years old and I've found it to be a positive experience—except when I have to pay it. If you're thinking of giving your children an allowance, keep the following in mind in order to make the practice as educational for them as it is costly for you.

1. Whatever the size of the allowance, children should be encouraged to divide their money into spending, charity and savings. You want them to learn to spend wisely. You want them to learn that generosity can make a positive difference in the world. And you definitely want them to learn to save for the future. You might need their help someday.

2. Pay the allowance on a weekday. If you wait for the weekend, your children are more likely to bring their cash along on errand runs and outings. Just having money in their pockets will make them more likely to find something to buy wherever they go—the grocery store, the hardware store, the post office. Give them the allowance on Monday and by Saturday they may forget to bring it along. Then when they say, "Look at this!" you can say, "Darn! And you without your wallet."

3. Still, you must eventually let children spend their spending money, not that it's easy to stand by silently as they buy Super Ooze or plastic handcuffs. And it's downright painful to see them spend real money on a package of fake money, which children have been known to do.

    My son once spent part of his allowance on a set of cheap plastic western toys. Along with the horse and cowboy there was a rock—a plastic rock. I've found enough real rocks in his pockets to gravel my driveway. It hurt me to see him spend money that was once mine on a plastic one. But parents can take comfort in the fact that when the money is gone and the toy is lost, broken or no longer interesting, the child will learn a valuable lesson from the most effective teaching method there is: the big mistake.

4. Stick with it. This isn't as hard as you think because your children will always remind you when it's allowance day. And eventually your consistency will pay off. The day will come when your kids have more money in their piggybanks than you have in your wallet. Be proud of all you've taught them about financial responsibility—but not too proud to borrow from them.

Daycare is For Babies, and You Can't Make Me Go Anymore

Every child with two employed parents will eventually march up to those parents and declare the following: "I've decided that I don't need childcare this summer. I am now old enough and mature enough to handle the challenges of being home all summer without supervision." My son made this announcement several years ago and I think what he actually said was, "Daycare is for babies, and you can't make me go anymore."

We mothers realize that children can't be expected to attend daycare for as long as we once thought was necessary—right up until they go off to college. And we recognize that as they become more independent, they also learn valuable lessons that will shape them into responsible adults who can take care of themselves and possibly us as well.

Naturally, we worry in the beginning of this new adventure but we soon learn that our children will be in contact with us throughout the summer—constant contact. I can't speak for fathers, but working mothers receive up to 500 phone calls from each of their children each day. These calls range from the predictable (I'm bored), to the alarming (where do you keep the Febreze?), to the interesting (did you know that women have more sweat glands than men, but men's are more active?). (No, I did not, but I did suspect it.)

Because kids who have hungered for more independence for years may be tempted to celebrate their new found freedom by lounging in front of the television for hours at a time, a responsible mother sets strict limits on screen time. She understands that relying on children to enforce those limits is a little like leaving the gate open and telling the pigs to stay out of the garden, but she also knows the parent/child relationship is built on trust—and on siblings' tattling.

The wise mother will also assign chores in order to keep the children occupied, teach responsibility and get out of doing those particular tasks herself. But she soon discovers that while she doesn't have to do them, she may have to re-do them, since the majority of chores will have been started and finished just as she is pulling into the driveway.

She will also notice that for every chore done, several others will have been created. For example, while the clean laundry has been put away there are dirty clothes lying all over the house. It turns out that preteens and teenagers change clothes more often than runway models.

And while the dishwasher has been unloaded, reloaded and started, there is a giant pile of dirty dishes waiting. On the bright side, this is a sign that the children are taking on the responsibility to make their own meals—or at least to make their own pasta. Surveys (done by me) show that pasta makes up approximately 81 percent of all food prepared by people under the age of 18. (The other 19 percent is made up of prepackaged food that is heated up in the microwave.)

It is at this stage in her children's development that Mom begins to go to bed before they do each night. They no longer need to be "tucked in" and she understands that their body clocks are shifting into teenage mode. Besides, she can't keep her eyes open, her own clock having done some shifting as well.

Before she retires for the night she warns her children that the later they stay up, the later they will sleep, and the later they sleep the later they will stay up, and so on, until that stressful morning when school begins. She knows that at that point, it will take a twenty-one gun salute and a bucket of ice water to get them out of bed, and twenty-one gun salutes are hard to come by, though ice water is not.

Ice water or not, the kids will be tired for those first few days of school. But mom will go to work pleased and satisfied that they are a little wiser and a little more self-reliant than they were when summer vacation began—and that she'll be getting a lot fewer phone calls at work.

IV
Over-Scheduled Child
Ever-Tired Mom

You're Going to Be in Everything and You're Going to Like It

New parents have so many decisions to make: cloth or disposable diapers, formula or mother's milk, soccer or Little League.

It's true. Children are starting competitive sports earlier and earlier these days. Many of them are still holding hands on the field—with the competition.

Part of the reason for this phenomenon is that we parents see our children as little packages of perfect potential. And if they never become Olympic athletes, it will be because we didn't sign them up for the right sports early enough.

Every day I drive by a tennis court on my way to and from work, and during the summer I often see children taking tennis lessons. I swear some of the kids are no taller than their rackets. When my son was that small, he used a tennis racket as a guitar, a baseball bat and a rifle. I'm not sure he ever hit an actual tennis ball with it until he was in elementary school—though he did use it on a golf ball once. And it's my fault because I didn't sign him up for tennis until he was at least nine. Or guitar lessons, or shooting lessons, or golf lessons.

We parents feel tremendous pressure (mostly from each other) to have our children succeed at activities we didn't succeed at, or did succeed at, or didn't even try but wish we would have. So, at great personal cost, we sign them up early and we sign them up

-99-

often. We put them in everything. The problem is, we don't teach them to drive.

So the whole family eats peanut butter sandwiches in the car between tee-ball and dance and spends summer vacation on the soccer field. We haul our children to this and that but we never actually see them—except from the bleachers and in the rear-view mirror.

In short, we over-book our children so they can be exactly like us—hurried, harried and tired. Only it took us years to become that way.

Those who have no children at home might wonder why a parent would assist their children with homework in the car on the way to drop off Child One at soccer and Child Two at gymnastics; pick up Child One and have him change in the car on the way to piano lessons; pick up Child Two (late) and drop her off at guitar lessons (late); stop to get gas; pick up Child One and feed him a peanut butter sandwich and chips in the car and have him change again on the way to Scouts; get groceries, especially peanut butter; pick up Child Two and feed her a peanut butter sandwich and chips in the car; take her to choir; clean the peanut butter and chips off the backseat; pick up both children; take them home and give them cold showers so they can stay awake long enough to finish their homework while she unloads the groceries, washes uniforms, makes sandwiches for tomorrow and crawls into bed after midnight.

Yes, a childless person might wonder why a parent would do that. A parent might wonder why she does that too. But truly, there are many logical reasons to over-schedule children.

- We were young once and we were superstars in every sporting event we ever participated in. And darn it, our children are going to do even better than we did and not only that, they're going to like it.
- Or, and this is more likely, we were benchwarmers in every sporting event we ever participated in. And darn it, our children are going to do better than we did and not only that, they're going to like it.
- Why should children have time to play? We don't.

- Home cooking isn't all it's cracked up to be, especially in some of our homes.
- If they work hard for the next five to ten years, our children might get scholarships. And after all the money we'll spend on traveling, uniforms and fund-raising candy bars, it's the least they can do.
- National parks are overrated. Meets and tournaments make perfectly fine family vacations.
- What with driving them all over town, we don't have time for our own fitness routine. They've got to learn the importance of regular exercise from someone.
- Our children are easier to get along with when we only have to see them from the bleachers.
- We like driving and we love fund-raising.
- Our family, neighbors and friends like having a reliable source for over-priced cookie dough, popcorn and extra-large candy bars.
- There is so much to be learned in competitive activities: that it's important to be a team player, that sportsmanship is a key to success and that adults throw temper tantrums too.
- We didn't have all of these opportunities available to us when we were growing up and see how we turned out.

The Beginnings of Baseball Players and Unattractive Parents

A friend told me, "Enjoy tee-ball. It's the last time kids' sports will be fun." When I protested, she told me that after tee-ball "the parents get ugly." Those were her words. "Some of them do, anyway," she said, "and it's enough to take the fun out of the game." She seemed to be hinting that I might be one of the uglier ones.

I vowed I would never "get ugly," at least not in the way she meant it. I may grow increasingly unattractive after sitting in the wind and the sun for hours. I may temporarily lose my composure when it's my turn to work the concession stand and thirty Little Leaguers show up at once, asking how much the hot dogs are but, I assured her, I would not "get ugly."

She was right about one thing, though. Tee-ball was fun, and it was fun from the moment we picked up Isaac's first "uniform," a baseball hat and a matching blue tee-shirt that came to his knees—a baseball dress.

Didn't matter. He wanted to wear it to school. He wanted to wear it to play. He wanted to wear it to bed. (Maybe I should have let him. It might have been easier to find it when we needed it.)

Letting two batches of six- and seven-year-olds loose on the field is like letting a bunch of cottontails loose on a golf course. Children were chatting and waving at their parents. They spun around and fell dramatically to the ground. They danced around with their gloves on their heads.

As my son did somersaults in the outfield during his first game, his coach hollered, "Everybody get ready!" One little boy said, "For what?"

I heard one father yell at his son, "Pay attention—and stop chewing your glove." Another boy started to run off the field during play. His dad called after him, "Where are you going?"

"I need a drink."

"Not now!"

By the second season, all the players were staying on the field for the entire game—though they weren't always standing at attention. Come to think of it, they weren't always standing at all.

In the beginning the kids were learning the fundamentals, like exactly which base is second and where the outfield is. The next year, they started working on the finer points, like how it's not necessary to slide into first base—or into the dugout. And while it's very important that you throw the ball, it's a bad idea to throw the bat.

In the beginning it took an excruciatingly long time for some children to hit the ball. When they did, it took an equally long time for them to realize the next thing to do is *run*! Meanwhile, the ball was rolling between many pairs of little feet. So it wasn't really a problem when the batter skipped to first base.

By the second season, there was no more skipping. There were a few saunters, and one near-cartwheel, but no skipping.

After my son's first hit of his baseball career, he actually ran—and even in the right direction. But then his batting helmet, which was three sizes too large, fell off. And what did he do? He ran back to get it. "That's great," I told my husband. "*Now* he's picking up after himself." His helmet didn't fit much better the second season, but he stopped running back to get it when it fell off.

He and the other players soon learned left field from right field. They stopped calling home plate "fourth base." And eventually they quit crossing it in pairs.

The kids have come a long way in a few short years. And just so you know, all the parents have behaved pretty darn well along the way. And that includes me, partly because my husband takes our turn in the concession stand.

Benched Again

Basketball is the perfect sport for many children because it allows them to do three of the things they love the most: run, jump and throw things.

That's one reason I was so happy that Isaac decided to play it. When it comes to running, jumping and throwing things, the gymnasium beats my house.

Besides, seeing him play brings back a lot of memories. I watched plenty of basketball when I was in school—and I had a perfect spot from which to see the action: the bench. During the three or four years I was on my high school's basketball team, I estimate I played a grand total of 12 minutes and 36 seconds. I sat on the bench so much I didn't even need to shower after the games. I often wished I'd brought my homework along so I could study while I sat there undisturbed. And more than once I was tempted to sneak away unnoticed to the concession stand—or to a restaurant downtown.

Truthfully, I didn't even feel that bad when we lost. I felt like I hadn't really played a part in how things turned out, so what did I care? But on those occasions when it appeared that my team was going to lose anyway, I wondered why I couldn't be allowed to help them do it. Because of course, I would have.

After all, there were legitimate reasons why I was on the bench. I wasn't a bad shot—as long as no one from the other team came anywhere near me. As you probably know, this is difficult to arrange. And every other aspect of the game eluded me, which is surprising when you consider how much time I spent watching it.

Needless to say, my basketball career was ho-hum. On the other hand, putting ten eight-year-olds on a basketball court is a lot like spilling a bucket of marbles on a just-waxed floor. Some players are so aggressive that they have no trouble stealing the ball—even from their own teammates. Others seem to be trying to figure out what role manners play in a basketball game. For example, if another player goes after the ball at the same time you do, should you take turns? If he tries to steal it from you, are you supposed to share?

And some players are downright manipulative. I'm not proud to admit that members of my son's team actually persuaded a player from the opposing team to shoot—at the wrong basket. Talk about succumbing to peer pressure! I only wish he'd made it.

It's fun, though. They don't keep score yet, so both sides can (and do) claim they won. We're still at the point where all the parents cheer for both sides and nobody yells at the coaches. This is probably because they don't want to be asked to take over.

And you can see the kids learning every week. Early in their basketball careers, they worked on the basics: dribbling and running (at the same time), shooting at the correct basket and not leaving the game to go to the bathroom.

Now that they've got a few seasons under their belts, they're working on the finer points, increasing their understanding of the rules and learning some plays. They understand clearly now that kicking the ball and tackling are for other sports. They've learned to guard their man—and that they should stop guarding their man when their team gets the ball back.

Meanwhile, I don't have nearly as good a seat to see the action as I did back when I was on the basketball team myself. But I'm having more fun watching.

The Elephant in the Living Room

We've all heard that a music education can help improve children's math and language skills and even enhance their brain development. It didn't work for me, but that hasn't kept me from believing that every child, mine included, should have music instruction.

That's why I was thrilled that, before I'd even tried to sell him on the idea, Isaac announced that he had decided to join the fourth grade orchestra. "Oh honey," I said, "that is wonderful news! Your dad and I were hoping you would want to play a musical instrument. Did you know that music will help you in all your other subjects? No? Well it will. I am so excited for you!"

Then he said, "I'm going to play the bass."

And I said, "Oh."

In case you don't know your stringed instruments, the bass is the big one. It's the elephant in the zoo that is a fourth grade orchestra. While Isaac would not be playing a full-size bass, he would be playing an instrument much larger than he is—a baby elephant.

As I'm sure you know, music education can be expensive, especially when you have to buy a larger vehicle to haul the instrument in. I'm kidding; we didn't get a new vehicle. But we should have.

One day shortly after he had made his announcement, Isaac was late coming out of the school. I was just beginning to get annoyed, as I am wont to do, when I saw my sixty-pound child coming slowly across the playground, lugging what looked like a dead body. Fortunately he had a friend to help him.

I had no friend to help me load the bass into the back of my Subaru Forester but I did have my son and two of his buddies to supervise. And it was not easy, especially with the supervising.

The bottom of the bass filled the entire storage space in my car; the neck lay over the seat and well into the passenger section where the boys sat, huddled together, afraid they'd suffer a head injury if I turned a corner too fast.

This was not the last time I would manage this maneuver. And while practice normally improves one's skills with a musical instrument, it did nothing to improve my skills getting it into and out of my car. I've only become increasingly irritable and more determined that my son take up the piccolo.

There is more room in my home than there is in my Subaru but there is still no place for an elephant, unless we remodel. So it sits in our living room, along with the music stand I used back in high school as last chair clarinetist.

And my son loves it. He loves the big noise it makes. He loves working on his correct bow hold and the proper positioning of his feet. He loves bowing after a "performance." "Can you see your shoes? Yes, I can see my shoes." In fact, he likes everything about the bass—except actually practicing it. I'm convinced he rosins his bow more than he uses it.

I realize that's not unusual behavior among young musicians. I think I spent half my practice time greasing the corks on my clarinet too. But I wouldn't mind hearing him practice the bass a little more than I do. Some parents cringe at practice time but, truly, the warm, low sounds emanating from a bass, even played by an inexperienced fourth grader, are not nearly as irritating as those coming from certain other instruments—say, my clarinet. But that was easier to haul.

Get Out Your Checkbook

Dear Friend, Neighbor, Coworker, Acquaintance or Perfect Stranger,

You may not remember this, but one day long ago—or not so long ago—your son or daughter, or maybe both, came to my home or called me on the telephone. He or she or they asked me to buy cookies or popcorn or wrapping paper or any number of other fundraising items for some very worthy cause.

As you and your kids soon learned, I'm a sucker for children—especially children selling treats. So is my husband. If they cornered us separately, we wound up with double of everything.

If you were with your child at the time, you assured me that I should not feel obligated. But I smiled and said, "No, I really want to." And I really did. I'm a parent too. I can't bear to see a small child rejected. Plus, deep down, I knew that someday my son would be the salesman.

So I placed my order and made out my check. Then I got out a long list I've been keeping and I wrote down your name.

For years I've been buying high quality but slightly overpriced candles and mixed nuts, Christmas wreaths and summer sausages, candy bars and greeting cards, all from somebody's children, quite possibly yours. And now ... it's your turn.

Get out your checkbook. Here he comes, my son Isaac, the Cookie Dough Salesman. We've been preparing for this day for a very long time. I've given him a lengthy list of qualified leads and I can assure you, your name is on it.

Don't argue with me. I have names, dates and a list of items I've purchased from your kids. And if that isn't enough, I can show you the stack of magazines in the corner I've never read, the year's supply of popcorn stored in my basement and the wrapping paper supply that will last me through the holiday season of 2050.

I admit I don't have any cookies, candy bars or chocolate covered nuts to show you. Those things don't last three days at my house. But I swear I did buy them. And I thoroughly enjoyed them, knowing that I was supporting the academic and/or extracurricular lives of young children, all while ensuring my own child's future sales success.

And so far he has been successful. He has just started his first sales campaign in what promises to be a lengthy career, and he's already nearing $100 in gross sales. I admit some of those sales were to me. Naturally I'm his best customer. And this new phase in my son's life just means I have one more child to buy from.

During his first-ever sales call to someone he doesn't live with, he sold $20 worth of cookie dough. Then he handed me the telephone so I could order $25 worth of mixed nuts from their child.

And unbelievably, while he was on the telephone with another potential sale, our doorbell rang. It was another child selling cookie dough. She remembered me from last year. What could I do?

Fundraising was and is part of the educational process for many of the kids I know, and it appears it will be for Isaac as well. That's all right. Children learn many valuable life lessons when they're out raising money.

They learn communication and math skills. They learn about hard work and goal setting. They learn how to deal with rejection and how to use the people in their life for financial gain. And they learn that turnabout is fair play. Now would you like chocolate chip or peanut butter?

Stay Calm and Don't Die: Lessons from the Car Pool

While there are many hazards to chauffeuring a carload of children, dozing off at the wheel isn't one of them. You could rear-end the car in front of you while you're looking into the backseat to see what just happened. You could drive off the road when one of the children says, "What does French kiss mean?" But you will never doze off. Or at least I never have.

For several years I've driven three boys, including my son Isaac, home after school every day. If you've never tried carpooling, you can get some sense of the experience by crawling into a tin can with a handful of firecrackers.

I'm learning a lot about children in general, and the children at my son's school in particular. For example, there's a boy there who can wiggle his ears and apparently spends a fair amount of time doing it. Even more remarkable, there is a child who can burp the ABCs. And according to my sources who have been monitoring the situation closely, there is a boy who went the entire school year without once blowing his nose. Impressive!

I know which children should be held back because they're having trouble and which ones will be held back because the teacher likes them too much to let them go. I know which kids pass gas, and

-111-

which ones visit the principal's office most often. (Oddly enough, none of my passengers are on any of these lists.)

I've learned who is in love with whom in third grade and I've learned how you can tell this is so: a girl likes a boy if she treats him like his mother would treat him. A boy likes a girl if he pretends to be hurt in order to get her to treat him like his mother does.

I've been reminded just how powerful a force peer pressure is. With a large enough dose of it, a boy can be persuaded to instantly change the career plan he's had his heart set on since kindergarten, taste food that's been rolling around on the floorboards for days and play a recorder with his nose.

I've learned that saying "hands to yourself" is not enough. If I really want to be effective, I have to be more specific. Keep your toes, feet, knees, hands, elbows, shoulders, chins, noses and foreheads to yourself!

I've learned some basic wisdom for life just by eavesdropping. For example, I've learned that parents should never wash out a child's mouth with soap because it can be toxic. I've learned that flapjacks are a form of gambling and that if you have eczema, you shouldn't eat eggs.

I now know that it's best to wear dark clothing. That way if you cut yourself the blood won't show. And if you ever find yourself in an emergency situation, you should "stay calm and don't die!"

And I've heard lengthy discussions on some thought-provoking questions: Which Yu-Gi-Oh! card trumps which? What happens when a teenager gets a pimple on top of a bruise? And are there or are there not bones in the tongue?

I've learned elementary school-aged boys excel at storytelling, one-upmanship and sound effects, especially disgusting sound effects. No, wait. I already knew that. But I was surprised to learn that they are also models of forgiveness. They can fight all the way to their drop-off point and still beg to play with each other after they get there. Thanks to the fighting, the answer will be "no." I guess I'm not as forgiving.

The Helicopter Parent's Guide to Camp

Isaac is at camp. It's not the first time he's been away from home without us, but it is the longest. If I didn't know it by the calendar, I'd know it by the smell of the hamster's cage.

Despite that and any misgivings I may have, I do understand that camp is good for both of us—my son and me, not the hamster. We're both in training after all, him to be more independent and me to let him be more independent.

Children challenge themselves both physically and mentally at camp. This prepares them for even greater tests later in their lives. They're away from parents, some for the first time. This builds confidence and self-reliance. They're living around many other campers. This prepares them to share a shower with fifty other people in a college dorm one day.

Parents learn while their children are away too. I've learned it's not necessary to buy a gallon of milk every time I go to the store. I find banana peels and empty cereal bowls scattered around and come to the painful realization that it's not just my son who doesn't pick up after himself. And I've learned that he apparently cleaned the hamster cage more often than I gave him credit for.

When children are away, every conversation between Mom and Dad begins with, "I wonder what he's doing now?" or "I hope she's

-113-

all right." We start to wonder what we talked about before we had children.

There are some good parts too: Nobody gripes about the dinner menu—except the cook. Nobody argues about bedtime and how much television is okay. And nobody complains about chores. Oh wait. I take that back.

Generally the house is peaceful and quiet and clean—relatively speaking. There is no one to set a good example for, so parents rent PG-13 movies and eat ice cream for breakfast if they want to. Well some of us do.

But the good parts are tempered with worry. Is he safe, having fun, behaving? Is she scared, lonely, homesick? And thanks to the wonders of modern technology, today's parents can see for themselves. Like many others, my son's camp has a Facebook page. We can spy! It's a helicopter parent's dream come true.

There are many videos and many more photos and I scan every one. I catch one split-second glimpse of him in a video. That's it? I scan them all again. Is that him in that large group of faces? Maybe. I guess he looks healthy and happy enough once I have my reading glasses on.

And what if he doesn't look happy? What if I stumble across a photo taken at the one and only moment when he looks miserable? I might assume he's homesick when really he just swallowed a mosquito or ate one too many s'mores. What would I do? Run to rescue him?

No, I would not. Difficult situations make us stronger. And not having fun is as much a part of life as having fun—and maybe more. I should know.

Instead, I'll eat whatever I want for breakfast. I'll buy less milk next time I go to the grocery store. I'll go on dates with my husband. And I'll clean the hamster cage. Or not.

V
Family Life is Like a Zoo
with the Lions Loose

Wise Mother Heads off Stressors

Certain times of the day are especially stressful for families with children. These include, but are not limited to, morning, after school, before dinner, after dinner and before bed. (Before you despair, remember there are those seven hours when the kids are in school.)

Wise mothers create a more peaceful family life by heading off each day part's particular stressors before they happen. According to one parenting article I read, a wise mother is up and ready for the day before she even thinks about waking the children. Apparently a wise mother is up before I am.

Even unwise mothers realize that children are harder to wake as they get older. I, for example, cannot lift my 13-year-old out of bed and toss him in the air anymore. And he doesn't giggle like he once did when I sing, "Here come the tickle bugs, sneaking up on you. They're looking for some breakfast; they think that you might do."

That's why wise mothers invest in loud, reliable alarm clocks for their older children. And they know that letting a child pick his own alarm clock will help him feel better about having to use one, at least until it goes off the first time.

The wise mother knows that starting the day right means taking time for breakfast, preferably together. But a hurried breakfast is better than no breakfast, and mothers who are not quite so wise sometimes find it necessary to allow the children to eat breakfast in the car. This rules out pancakes, but we never have time to make those anyway.

Wise mothers know that getting everyone out of bed on time does not guarantee leaving the house on time. Children have a way of coming up with urgent tasks while they're preparing for school— for example, picking up the toys they were told to pick up three days ago, or carefully writing, "I love you, Mom" in toothpaste on the bathroom wall. This leaves Mom in a tough spot at what is already a difficult time. The wise mother uses a diplomatic approach like, "Oh sweetie, I love you too. Now *get ready right this minute!* And plan on cleaning that up tonight."

Children are ravenous after school, and a wise mother knows that a hungry child is a grumpy child. A hungry mom is a grumpy mom too; that's why I'm wise enough to eat at my desk all day. Because children aren't allowed to do this, and because they're often rushing to activities after school, wise mothers carry nutritious snacks in the car. The really clever ones also cover the seats.

Wise mothers use drive time to listen to their children talk about their day and they encourage them to talk about their tomorrow as well. This heads off the common bedtime crisis where a child, ready to doze off, suddenly recalls she has a paper maché castle and medieval costume due the next morning.

When the family arrives home from after-school activities and errands, everyone is tired; but there's homework to be done and dinner to make. The wise mother handles dinner preparation with efficiency, grace and carry-out. Alternatively, she takes full advantage of leftovers and cream of mushroom soup.

She also wisely insists that all family members share in kitchen clean-up. She knows prompting them to help may not get the job done but it will remind them of all the homework they still have to do.

When the homework is finally done, the wise mother encourages her children to pack their lunches for the next day. She inspects what they've packed, though, since children can only live so long on Skittles and juice boxes.

She also encourages her children to lay out not only their clothes for the next day but their shoes as well. As a not-so-wise mother, I've spent up to twenty minutes hunting for shoes—my own.

Finally, the wise mother knows that children should go to bed early. If not, they should be quiet so that she can.

Princess Charlotte Elizabeth Diana of Cambridge, Don't Make Me Tell You Again

Royal babies sure have a lot more names than other babies have. I've never paid much attention to Britain's Royal Family before, but I couldn't help noticing all the fuss about the birth of Princess Charlotte Elizabeth Diana of Cambridge. If she has to sign every piece of homework she ever does with her full name, she's never going to get any recess.

It's a lovely name but I wonder if her parents ran it through the two tests for baby naming, the first one being the Angry Parent Test. Expectant parents should always test baby names by yelling the entire thing. They may be tempted to do it for real one day and they'll want it to be effective. By the time Duchess Kate finishes yelling "Princess Charlotte Elizabeth Diana of Cambridge, don't make me tell you again," neither one of them will remember what she's mad about.

The CEO Test ensures that parents don't choose a name that will limit the child's future career opportunities. I know it's not fair, but a name like Fizzle or Ham Hock might keep an employer from taking a job candidate seriously. Princess Charlotte Elizabeth Diana of Cambridge is distinguished enough to pass the CEO Test, but I've never seen a job application with space for it.

It's okay though. She already has a career. While I was reading up on the new princess, I learned that her official job title is Her Royal Highness Princess Charlotte of Cambridge, and a large part of her job description consists of being fourth in line to succeed Queen Elizabeth, after her grandfather, father and brother. It sounds like she's a lady in waiting to me, but maybe that's something else.

While I was royal watching, I saw a lot of photographs of the princess, her brother, her father and other relatives as youngsters. And photos of the royal family are as distinguished as their names are. Looking at them, you'd think royal babies don't cry, spit up or get baby acne. And royal siblings are either especially good at hiding their true feelings or they really aren't disappointed that they didn't get a puppy instead.

Conspicuously absent were the most common baby photos found in American photo albums. I saw no pictures of any royal child in the bathtub or covered in baby food. Every photo album I've ever seen has both of those. I don't recall what Isaac was eating when I took our baby food photo, but it must have been beets, tomatoes, or a combination of both because he looks like he just had a shaving accident, except he hadn't started shaving yet.

I also saw no photos of a royal baby lying on his or her father's chest as they both snooze. That's the other most common baby photo in American photo albums. You never see a photo of a new mom like that. Mothers don't sleep for the first two years of their children's lives and only for short spurts after that. I imagine Kate has hired help, so she may be able to catch a nap. We probably still won't see a picture of it, though.

In all the photos I found of Kate, she looked far too distinguished to be caught napping, and yet she looked better rested and more relaxed than most mothers of newborns. Or at least, better rested and more relaxed than I did when I had a newborn—and quite possibly than I have at any time since.

The Ill-Mannered, Obnoxious Babysitter

My son and his friend once sang "viva Viagra" from the backseat, all the way across town. One morning after I hadn't slept well, he suggested I try Lunesta. But when he told me he had just saved a lot of money on car insurance, it finally hit me: We need TV-Turnoff Week.

TV-Turnoff Week is a project of the TV-Turnoff Network, a nonprofit organization whose mission is to encourage children and adults to watch less television in order to improve our health and stop speaking in advertising slogans.

I read that American children watch an average of 19 hours and 40 minutes of television per week. This is more than any other activity except sleeping, and it explains why they don't have time to clean their rooms and do their math homework.

Speaking of math homework, if my math is correct (and it probably isn't), it also means that by the age of 18, children will have spent around two entire years of their young, impressionable lives watching television. That's two years when they could have been working for world peace, earning college money and cleaning, not only their room, but the entire house.

I watched TV as a child too. But I'm certain I didn't watch 19 hours of it every week. In my childhood home, there were ten children, one television and one channel. In other words, there was no place to sit and not much to watch if you did find a spot. I admit I didn't spend two years of my childhood working for world peace either, but I may still get to that.

My son doesn't watch 19 hours of television per week either, but he watches plenty. He must; he pops a stick of gum in his mouth and raves about "minty freshness." After a particularly graphic TV commercial, he said with enthusiasm, "I'm glad I don't have bladder problems!" And it was TV advertising that convinced him we should buy a metal detector. "You could lose weight," he said.

"Do I need to lose weight?" He said nothing, so I went on, "Anyway, that's not why people buy metal detectors."

"They lose weight," he pointed out patiently, "because they walk around carrying a metal detector while they're looking for treasure."

I told him I walk around plenty without a metal detector and I haven't lost any weight. I haven't found any treasure either.

And it isn't just my son. After seeing our garage, one of his friends suggested I watch "Garage Takeover" weekdays on the Discovery Channel. I took this as an insult but he said he was only trying to help.

I know television isn't all bad. While watching favorite shows together, children and parents can bond with each other as their butts bond to the couch.

Most busy parents, including this one, have at one time or another resorted to using television as a babysitter. And it is a cheap babysitter, albeit an ill-mannered, obnoxious one. But it certainly is not a free babysitter—not if you count cable and the cost of sugary cereals and metal detectors.

And television does offer some educational programming. My son can speak endlessly about World War II and Bigfoot. And he learned how to crack open a coconut by watching a survival show. You never know when you might come across a coconut.

Character Building in the Bathroom

The number of children in any family is inversely proportional to the number of bathrooms in their home. More children, fewer bathrooms. Large families simply have more important things to spend their money on—groceries, for example.

I speak from experience. I grew up in family of ten children and one bathroom. Oh yes, and one hot water heater. I don't know how big it was, but I know it wasn't big enough. My husband, son and I live in a home with an ample hot water heater and not one, not two, but three bathrooms. One for each of us.

While it's true we have more company than a hotel on Maui, three bathrooms seem extravagant even to me. I can only use one at a time. Obviously the builder of our home spent even more of his childhood waiting than I did.

Now that I no longer live with the drawbacks of one bathroom, though, I'm finally beginning to appreciate just how much I learned from the experience—in the same way veterans say they learned a lot during a war.

A large family provides a wealth of learning experiences anyway. Children with many siblings learn to answer to any name and eat fast if they want seconds. They learn to value solitude which, incidentally, can only be found in the bathroom, though there is no guarantee of it there either. And they learn to honor the large family's unique brand of hospitality known as "on your feet, lose your seat." But the lessons learned sharing one bathroom are by far the most valuable.

Girls who grow up in a family of seven brothers and one bathroom, as I did, learn to take nothing for granted; toilet seat up is standard operating procedure. Boys and girls who grow up in homes with many children and one bathroom learn about being patient—and assertive when necessary. They learn about putting others first—especially if the others are bigger than they are. They learn to conserve hot water. And they learn to plan ahead. There is nothing spontaneous about taking a shower in a large family.

To maintain peace in the home, it is essential that the would-be bather declare his or her intentions to everyone else in the family before locking the bathroom door to make sure no one has more pressing business. Thanks to the wisdom that comes with age, I finally understand why my entire family laughed at me each time I thoughtfully announced, "Everyone get in the bathroom. I'm taking a shower."

Children living with one bathroom learn about taking turns, or finding creative ways to avoid taking turns. One of my sisters and I devised a scheme whereby we would get "our share" of the hot water and then some. One of us would leave the bathroom door unlocked while we took our shower. The other would sneak in while no one was looking—no easy task—and step into the shower just as we were stepping out. We'd leave the water running so our siblings wouldn't know they'd just missed their turn. I'm still amazed at how long this worked before one of my brothers caught on, slipped into the basement and turned off the hot water heater in the middle of my shower.

All of these character-building lessons shaped my siblings and me in ways no summer camp could have. It's unfortunate my son is going to miss out on all of them. As an only child in a home with three bathrooms, the only bathroom-related lesson I foresee him learning is how to make a decision...and how to clean a bathroom.

Do No Harm. Or, at Least, Don't Do Much Harm

In every household, there is an unsung hero, one brave soul who has gained the title of family chef, either because she or he likes to cook or because nobody else will. I am that hero in my home, though my family has never once called me that.

As chefs for the family, we have the difficult job of balancing the time available to prepare meals and the affordability and nutritional value of ingredients with the preferences of all family members. (Family chefs talk about their family's "preferences" because it's nicer than saying they're "picky.")

There is at best a 31-second window between the time we arrive home from our day jobs and the time the children begin asking, "What's for supper?" But if time were the only factor we would pick up carryout every day. Too much of that and we would have to forgo some of life's other luxuries, for example electricity and phone service.

But if affordability and speed were the only issues, we would serve a certain inexpensive noodle, whose main ingredient is sodium, for every meal.

Naturally we also hope to feed our families something nutritious. And besides, we have taken the Family Chef's Oath: Do no harm. Or at least, don't do much harm. Some of the fastest and most affordable meals we know are loaded with trans fat, sugar and artificial flavorings, and have as much nutritional value as chewing gum. But if good health were the only issue we would serve skinless chicken breasts, steamed broccoli and flax flakes more often.

As informed family chefs, we know that no nutrients are absorbed through the skin when children play with their food. (Unless they're sitting on the deck on a sunny day soaking up vitamin D while they sword fight with their asparagus spears.)

Likewise we realize that, even if we prepare a meal in seven minutes, no time is saved if the family stares at their plates for half an hour. And if we cook an inexpensive meal and no one but the dog eats it, no money is saved—except on dog food.

Besides, after all the stress we endure to prepare nutritious meals within budget and time constraints, we deserve something delicious even if nobody else in the family does.

Balancing all of these issues often drives the desperate family chef to the cookbook collection. This is almost always a mistake. As we gaze at the beautiful photographs our mouths begin to water and we are overcome by optimism. We start to think that not only will we be able to find saffron, we'll be able to afford it. We convince ourselves that yes, we have time to brine a pork roast or roll chicken breasts around a mixture of chopped mushrooms, spinach and cheese, and what's more, we'll feel like doing it when the time comes.

Some cookbooks even go so far as to claim, "The kids will love it!" Besides being an outright lie, this exploits our hunger for appreciation and anything that isn't macaroni. We begin to believe that the same children who think peanut butter is a delicacy will eat and enjoy the Burmese Chicken Curry with Yellow Lentils.

We may even go so far as to pick up the ingredients for the Walnut Crusted Potato and Blue Cheese Cakes. And because on those rare occasions when we have time we really do enjoy cooking, we might even look forward to making it.

But then there are piano lessons, basketball practice and fish sticks in the freezer.

Family Chefs unite! In response to the struggles we face every day family chefs simply must avoid cookbooks that do not balance all that we must balance. We must expect the praise and appreciation of our families—not to mention that they clean up the kitchen after meals. And we must demand that they take us out to dinner a lot more often.

Hotdish a la King Again?

There are many ways to save time in the kitchen—besides the one that comes to mind first for most of us: eating out of the kettle you cooked in.

Saving time in the kitchen actually begins way back at the grocery store when you're stocking up on "staples." As you know, flour and sugar were once considered staples. Not anymore. Those involve baking. Always remember, if you never use your oven you never have to clean your oven. Also you'll never set off your smoke alarm.

Today, spaghetti sauce and cream of something soups are staples for the busy cook. The variety in my family's diet is limited only by the number of cream of something soups there are available, and there are many. Cream soups are miracle workers at saving time and stretching ingredients when you have a houseful to feed. In fact—and you probably read this—biblical scholars now believe that cream of mushroom soup was likely involved in the feeding of the five thousand.

To really save time in the kitchen, though, you must learn to make the most of leftovers. Some cooks insist that certain foods are even better the second time they're served. Careful observation will reveal these are usually the people who cooked them.

As the main cook at my house, I'd go so far as to say some foods are better the third or fourth time around. In my opinion the benefits of serving leftovers far outweigh the benefits of cooking something fresh—especially if I'm doing the cooking.

Certainly I save both cooking and dishwashing time, since we can store, heat and eat from the same dish. We only have to plan meals every three or four days. And the family doesn't waste nearly as much time eating.

Those of us who are unencumbered by good taste also save money—which we can spend eating out. And we save calories. No one ever overindulges in recycled goulash or tuna surprise. (They may not overindulge in the originals either.)

Unwelcome guests rarely return. (And if they do, they bring food.) And with careful planning and an ample supply of freezer bags, we can freeze enough leftovers between Thanksgiving and New Year's Day to last through the Fourth of July.

But to enjoy all these benefits, if not at mealtime, you must somehow convince your family to eat the leftovers you serve. Here are some tips that, while not doing much in the way of flavor enhancement, might dupe them into eating:

1. Give it a new look. For example, on day number two, you could sprinkle some cheese on that meat loaf. On day number three, scrape it back off.

2. Never admit that you're serving leftovers. If anyone asks why that main dish showed up again, say "It didn't. I thought I'd whip up another batch since the first one went over so well." (Oh yes, and did they notice? This time, you tried it with cheese on top.)

3. Canned soup is a leftover entrée's best friend. Cream of Something Soup, plus rice or pasta, plus leftover meat equal exciting new hotdish. Exciting new hotdish plus canned broth equal exciting new soup. I could go on, but you'd probably rather I didn't, especially if it's close to lunch time.

4. Make it a household rule that he who complains cooks the next meal. I'm amazed at the things my husband has not complained about in my effort to get him to complain. My son

still complains, however; he knows I don't trust him with the gas stove yet.

5. Empathize, but not with your family. If they ask why that roast keeps coming back, tell them you felt sorry for it.

6. Be careful what you call it. Children are programmed to spit out anything with the words "leftover" in the name. If you really want them to eat, try using elegant-sounding culinary terms like "a la king" and "hash." This may be slightly more effective than saying, "Then I guess you'll just have to go hungry." (But probably not.)

7. You must also avoid using the same name for the same dish too often. For example, if you called it "casserole" on Wednesday, call it "hotdish" on Thursday.

8. Everyone deserves a second chance. The fact that a particular entree wasn't that tasty the first time around doesn't mean it won't get better with age.

9. Enough is enough. There comes a day when all good things must end. (Bad things too.) A rule of thumb is that it goes in the trash when even the dog is tired of it.

10. And finally, and most importantly, as the chef in your home, you may have to cook it, store it, warm it and smile as you set it before your family, but there's no law that says you have to eat it.

You Do Not Need a Plate for Pie

Dishwashing is a meditative activity, maybe because it is so often a solitary one. And I've had a lot of time to meditate lately. My dishwasher resigned without giving notice, leaving me to think and scrub and contemplate and rinse far more than I normally care to.

One of the many issues I've pondered while I've been standing at the sink is this: how can my small family dirty so many dishes? More importantly, how could we dirty fewer of them?

Fortunately I've had plenty of time to think up some answers. We could eat out more. And when we eat in, I could more closely monitor my family's dish use: "Hey! You only drank out of that glass once. I don't care if it was yesterday." "You do not need a plate for pie!"

I also thought back to how much I wanted a dishwasher when I was growing up. There were ten children in my family and ten children dirty a lot of dishes. But my parents maintained that they didn't just have ten children, they had ten dishwashers. And besides, back then the mechanical dishwashers weren't all that efficient. But then, neither were their ten dishwashers.

I recall that the perceived need to "soak" the pots and pans could get us out of washing them for days. I've noticed quite a lot of soaking going on at my house lately too. I also remember that there

-131-

were many arguments about whose turn it was to wash dishes. But a dishwasher probably wouldn't have eliminated the arguments; we would have fought over whose turn it was to load it.

It was also while I was washing dishes that I came to a profound realization: I need bigger cupboards. I had no idea how many dishes I was storing in my dishwasher until I couldn't store them there anymore. It's possible that some of my plates and glasses have until now never seen the inside of my cupboards. They've gone from the dishwasher to the table and back again day after day, year after year. A dishwasher is a good place to store dishes just like a dryer is a good place to store clothing. And no matter how long you leave the dishes in the dishwasher, they never wrinkle.

But what I've thought about—stewed about, fumed about—the most while I've been washing dishes is all the people I know who wash their dishes before their dishwasher washes their dishes. This has always annoyed me, especially now that I have no choice in the matter.

I don't go as far as a young man I know who once left the chicken bones on the plates when he put them in the dishwasher. But I sincerely believe the smears of spaghetti sauce and the rings of hot chocolate are signals to my family. Really.

Think of it this way: What if someday when I have a dishwasher again, I start rinsing the dishes before I load the dishwasher. This is unlikely, but what if I do? And what if someone comes by before I run the dishwasher and, thinking the dishes are clean because they look clean, takes them out of the dishwasher and puts them away (not that anyone would actually do this)? But theoretically it is possible that we could eat our next meal off dirty dishes that look clean.

Then again, so what if we do? If the dishes look clean enough to eat off before they've been run through the dishwasher, why run them through the dishwasher? And that's precisely my point. If your dishwasher really needs you to wash the dishes before it washes the dishes, what do you need your dishwasher for? Unless you just need some time to think, in which case would you like to come to our house to do it?

Another Garage Sale Foiled

There comes a moment in the life of every family, when someone declares it's time to downsize. Usually this is the parent with the fewest belongings.

Other family members don't usually react enthusiastically to the suggestion, so the inspired parent appeals to their higher motives. "Wouldn't it be nice to give away the things we don't need any more to people who do need them?" No one is persuaded, partly because they think they still need almost everything, and what they don't need, they want.

She tries another tack. She tells them she read that Americans spend 150 hours each year trying to find belongings in their homes. She points out that it might be easier to find what they need if they didn't have to wade through so much of what they don't need. "Just think, another 150 hours to play!"

"But," the children argue, "we won't have anything left to play with."

She appeals to baser motives. She suggests they sell everything they don't need—or want—at a garage sale and make some extra cash. "Then we could buy more!" says a child.

And that settles it. They begin sorting their possessions optimistically, dollar signs in their eyes. But then they come across items they'd forgotten they even owned, and they remember with a pang how special these once were. They recall the adventure they were on when they bought the talking trout or the kindness of the person who gave them the Mickey Mouse waffle maker. How can they possibly part with it? Belongings that have been under the bed covered with dust bunnies are transferred to places of honor on crowded shelves.

Someone remembers reading that a ponytail brunette Barbie made in 1959 is now worth more than $10,000. Suddenly a slightly balding doll with pen marks for jewelry becomes the college fund. They forget that Barbie was still hermetically sealed in her box, and that this doll has been lying in the corner of the moldy basement for four years. It's carefully wrapped in tissue paper, though, and moved to the top shelf of the linen closet.

Many other potential giveaways are foiled by those five little words, "I might need it someday." The instigator of the cleanup begins to panic. "If it's so darn useful, why has it been in the crawl space covered in spider webs since we moved in twelve years ago?"

The finder counters, "If I'd known we had it, I would have been using it." This is how power cords for unknown devices, parts for long lost gadgets, jars without lids, and lids without bowls find their way back onto cluttered shelves. At least they're up off the floor— for now.

Other things are too important to throw away. What if the IRS wants to see the receipt for the computer keyboard purchased a decade ago? Or what if the current owner of the car they sold five years ago wants to see the maintenance schedule? They decide to keep them for now—to throw away later.

By now the downsizing effort has completely degenerated. When the parents aren't looking the children snatch broken toys from the trash. And when the children aren't looking the parents grab the children's discarded toddler toys and tattered baby blankets from the giveaway box—for the grandkids.

In the end, all the hours, sweat and arguments result in one small stack in the middle of the living room. Unfortunately, it's not nearly enough for a garage sale. What to do?

They decide to store it until there's more.

VI
Don't Bother Me!
I'm Busy Writing a Book about
Good Parenting

Celebrating the Finder in Chief

This essay is dedicated to all those mothers who worry that if they leave town, their family will have to go next door to use the bathroom because they won't know where to find more toilet paper when the roll is empty.

On Mother's Day we celebrate not only all that mothers are and do, but all they know. Moms know the health history, food preferences, idiosyncrasies, sleep habits, social calendar and work schedule of every member of the family. They know everyone's birth weight, birth date and birthday cake preference. And they know the whereabouts of clothing, electronics, text books and other paraphernalia dropped by family members who go through the house shedding belongings like overdressed tourists in the desert.

With so much to remember it's no wonder mothers occasionally put wet clothes in the dryer and forget to turn it on. It's no wonder they sometimes put the cereal in the refrigerator and the milk in the cupboard—the bathroom cupboard. And it's no wonder they try six names before they get to the one belonging to the person they're speaking to. (And some of them are names of people they don't even know.)

Moms simply have too much on their minds. They know too much. Let's focus on one aspect of this great knowledge: a mother's amazing instinct for knowing the whereabouts of every family member's belongings, or at least their unshakeable belief that she does. Mom is the Finder in Chief for the whole family.

Every third sentence she hears from other family members begins with, "Have you seen my...," as in, "Have you seen my sweatshirt, cell phone, math homework or half-eaten peanut butter and jelly sandwich?" Sometimes there's an edge to the question, as though the asker really means, "What did you do with my sweatshirt, cell phone, math homework or half-eaten peanut butter and jelly sandwich?" They're careful, though. They may not know where to find anything in the house but they do know it's bad manners to insult the locals before you ask for directions.

The Finder in Chief also has exclusive knowledge of the location of all necessities stored in the home. Family members who go through entire rolls of paper towels daily will do without them until Mom gets more from the pantry, or the basement or wherever they've been stored since the family moved into their home fifteen years ago. Tissue boxes will remain empty on the shelf until she goes to the cupboard for new ones, even if the whole family has the crud.

Children who are normally diligent about handwashing will do without soap until Mom refills the soap dispenser. They simply do not know where these things are. And if they do they're not saying.

Being the Finder in Chief can be exhausting, which may help to explain the great irony of the job. A mother who has reloaded all the paper product dispensers in the house, then located a missing shoe in the back seat of the car, a science worksheet under the couch and a contact lens in the carpet, will not be able to find her own car keys. And there is no one to help her.

Here is my wish for all you Finders in Chief on Mother's Day. May you eventually manage to impart your great wisdom and skill to your family. But on Mother's Day at least, might no one ask for it. May you put the milk in the refrigerator and the cereal in the cupboard. And may you find your reading glasses, or your other black shoe or whatever it is you're missing. Better yet, may some kind family member find it for you.

Get Yourself a Man Purse

During her child-rearing years, a woman's handbag expands like a maternal belly. And it isn't just the coloring book, the animal crackers and the assortment of toys she keeps on hand for emergencies. Her husband, the same man who teases her about the size and weight of her bag, is forever asking her, "Honey, could you put this in your purse?" Then he'll hand her his candy wrapper. Or his sunglasses. Or his tire iron.

We, the so-called weaker sex, carry the belongings of our entire family on one shoulder. We wouldn't do it if there weren't a really good reason. It's the old Scout motto: be prepared. I'm surprised more Boy Scouts don't carry purses.

Since the birth of my son seven years ago, my handbag has been well stocked with snacks, wipes, toys, crayons, paper and some amazing stain-removing towelettes. I never have much money but I do have little green army men. You never know when you might need an army man—maybe to help you lift your purse.

I carry everything my family could need or want, though quite often I can't find my car keys amongst it all. And misplaced car keys and the changing of the seasons are my two major motivations for cleaning out my handbag.

Each spring and fall I transfer the contents of my purse into another more suited to the season. In my pre-child days, when fashion meant more to me than function, this was a matter of style. Now it just seems prudent that at least twice a year, I should remove the rubbish that has accumulated.

The last time I cleaned my purse I found, among other things, a bill I thought I paid months ago; a set of keys I thought I was missing; expired coupons worth $12.50; an assortment of candy and gum wrappers, several containing chewed gum; and a petrified hotdog wrapped in a napkin. I'm just glad Isaac doesn't like mustard and pickle relish.

Eventually my handbag falls apart under the strain and I go shopping for a new one. I can't help but gaze longingly at the slim, chic versions. But I'm painfully aware that those are for single childless women who are never forced to quickly dispose of a half-eaten peanut butter sandwich; who never, at a moment's notice, find themselves entertaining a carload of children; and who never have to blow their own nose, let alone wipe anyone else's.

In the past practicality has always prevailed and I have traded up to an even larger model. Even so, I haven't zipped, clasped or in any other way been able to close a purse in years. This is a problem since, by now, mine is large enough to check when I fly.

But one day recently while I was browsing through the handbags at a local department store, I realized how very tired I am of carrying the weight of my world. And I made a rash decision: my husband and son can carry their own purses. They will be uncomfortable with the idea, but I'll appeal to their masculinity. What could be more manly than carrying your own belongings?

I'll encourage them to call their purses by another name if it makes them feel better. Maybe "satchel" or "pocketbook" sounds more masculine. What about "clutch?" *Vroom! Vroom!*

Before I could change my mind I picked out a new handbag, a sleek little number with slim zippered pockets. There is no room for trash or toys or tools in this purse. It is stylish, even elegant. And it's just the right color for spring: Vanilla Cream, they call it.

I took it home and loaded it up. It is lovely.

But I can't get the darn thing to zip.

Nonsense and Momsense

I told Isaac he could get a cell phone as soon as he proved he was responsible enough to take care of it. Then I misplaced mine. Luckily he was able to find it for me—in the garbage can in the garage.

If that weren't bad enough, he hadn't even had his own phone a year when I washed it in the washing machine. Naturally he was a little perturbed. I told him it wouldn't have happened if he did the laundry, to which he replied, "Take responsibility for your actions, Mom." Where did he hear that?

Half the time our kids don't seem to listen, and when they do, they act like they don't believe us anyway. But then when we least expect it, they pipe up and use our own wise words against us. For example I've told my son repeatedly that he should always finish what he starts. Then one day I quit a computer football game we were playing. "You should always finish what you start," he said. I told him I hadn't wanted to play the stupid game in the first place; I hate football; and the darn computer game was taking longer than a real one. "Don't make excuses, Mom." Oh yeah.

When he was younger and I was smarter, he and I had a lovely, heartfelt discussion about the conscience. Several days later he informed me that his conscience had told him not to eat cooked

-140-

broccoli. But when I turned up my nose at a dessert he'd created using peanut butter and Nesquik, he reminded me that I should be willing to try new foods.

That's what makes passing our hard-earned wisdom on to our children so challenging. How can we teach them to do as we say when we don't do as we say? Or at least I don't. Quite often I catch myself telling my son to stop yelling in the house—by yelling in the house.

I tell him that it's important that we pay our bills on time but I'm not sure I'd pay his allowance on time if he didn't remind me. I may not ever pay his allowance at all if he didn't remind me. It's just that I don't always have cash on hand. I know; don't make excuses.

I cut off a telemarketer the other night by saying in my best breathless, hurried voice, "Sorry. I can't talk. I'm just headed out the door." I wasn't breathless, hurried or headed out the door, but I thought that was nicer than what I wanted to say. Nice or not, when I hung up the phone Isaac said, "You aren't going anywhere. You lied!" Oh. Thanks for pointing that out.

Our children could get the impression watching us that they should never say naughty words—except in traffic; that they should always speak kindly of others—unless they disagree with them politically; and that they should always respect their elders—except for the referees at professional sporting events.

We tell them to go get some fresh air and exercise—from our place on the couch. We tell them not to talk on the cell phone when they drive—even if we do. We tell them patience is a virtue; then we lose ours. Or at least I do, and fairly often too.

And that, I suppose, is an excellent time to teach them that nobody is perfect. I think they'll see the wisdom in that.

Life in the Chicken Coop

At times, my only child has expressed a desire to have a sibling—or a pet. Either one. I had both pets and siblings when I was growing up—a lot of them. And while I never once regretted the pets, I have to admit there were times I wished I didn't have the siblings. I'd feel guilty saying that if I wasn't so sure they've felt the same way on a few occasions. I often indulged in a childhood fantasy in which I lived alone in the chicken coop we had in our backyard—without the chickens. In my daydream my parents brought me meals and none of my nine siblings ever entered unless I invited them. Pets were always welcome, though.

Today I count my siblings among my dearest friends and feel blessed to have grown up in a large family. As number nine of ten, who is also the mother of an only child, I have a unique perspective on family size. And I have to say that life for an only child is no better or worse than life for children of large families. But it is vastly different.

Children from large families learn responsibility early by caring for younger siblings. (Not that I did, being number nine. I'm still learning responsibility.) Only children learn to take responsibility for their actions early, simply because there is no one else to blame—unless it's a parent. (And it sometimes is.)

Children from large families long for the day they'll have their own bedrooms. Only children complain about having to sleep alone.

Children from large families always have someone to play with—even if it is just a sibling. Only children think they should always have someone to play with too—even if it's just a parent.

Children from large families argue, bicker and debate with each other. Only children argue, bicker and debate with their parents.

Children from large families look for ways to stand out among the crowd and be noticed by their parents. Only children look for ways to lie low and avoid being noticed by their parents.

Children from large families learn to answer to anything, having frequently been called six or eight names before the parent gets to them. I have never called my son six or eight names before getting to his, though I have called him by his father's name and the name of the boy down the street.

Children from large families spend lots of time with siblings, occasionally picking up naughty words and bad habits from them. Only children spend more time with their parents, occasionally picking up naughty words and bad habits from them.

Children of large families learn to eat fast if they want seconds. Only children learn to eat out.

As adults, only children will have no one to fight with over the inheritance. As adults, children from large families will have no inheritance to fight over.

Only children have occasional bouts of loneliness to deal with. This helps to build character but can also lead to unrealistic fantasies about siblings and pets. Children from large families crave solitude. This helps build character too, but can also lead to unrealistic fantasies about life in a chicken coop.

I Should Be Better at This

My parents raised ten children in a three-bedroom house with one bathroom. And they did it without a cell phone, a mini-van or a reality show. They were remarkable, and I could have learned a great deal from them if I were the type to catch on.

I mean no offense to any other mother, but I've actually heard women say with great trepidation, "*Oh no*! I'm becoming my mother." Don't worry. That wasn't your daughter. Nor was it my daughter, but only because I don't have a daughter.

I wish I could be more like my mother. Coincidentally my son also wishes I could be more like my mother. Unfortunately the apple not only fell far from the tree, it rolled down the hill and across the street.

I wish I'd learned to stay cool under pressure like she did. When I was a child I watched her prepare more food for every meal than I cook in three days. I watched her kill a rattlesnake that was coiled up in the yard near where I was playing. It didn't stand a chance. I watched her pull a needle out of my thumb after I sewed over it with the sewing machine. I quit sewing shortly after that.

If I had watched my mother more closely I would have learned how to be patient with the shortcomings of others. Out of all the possible explanations for someone's behavior she always chose the one that left her feeling the least slighted. "They're busy. They're tired. They forgot." I never once heard her say, "Idiots!" which I say several times a day. She never gossiped or trashed the reputation of others and she didn't join in when those around her did, no matter how hard I tried to get her to.

Mom was never one to spout platitudes like "eat your vegetables" or "wear clean underwear in case you're in an accident." I think she figured if we wore the same underwear two days in a row it meant less laundry. And if one of us wouldn't eat the carrots, somebody else would. We knew that too, so we ate the carrots.

One big lesson my son wishes I learned from my mother is that once your kids leave home you're no longer "the boss of them." You don't get to tell them to clean their rooms anymore, or eat their vegetables or come in by midnight—unless they move out when they're eight years old. You can try to tell them but you shouldn't be surprised if they don't listen—and if they don't seem happy to see you.

Another lesson my son hopes I learned from my mother is that it's best not to offer unwanted advice to your adult children—and maybe nobody else either. The magical result of my mother never giving unsolicited advice is that her children often solicited it, calling long distance to ask her how to make gravy without lumps or sauerkraut casserole, though not all our spouses fully appreciate that.

I'm not speaking about *your* children of course, but did you know there are adults who dread their mother's visit because they don't want her checking for dust bunnies under the bed or criticizing their spouse? And they're afraid she'll ask when they're going to have children or when they're going to have *more* children My mother lived with me for years and she never once criticized my housekeeping, my parenting or my cooking. If you've seen my housekeeping or eaten my cooking, you might find this hard to believe, but it's true. Plenty of other visitors have criticized all of the above. I don't invite them back.

I suppose I'm more like my father. From him, I inherited my insomnia, my nose, my sense of humor and my sense of humor about my nose.

My dad managed the water department in the small town in which we lived. He spent his vacations assisting area ranchers during lambing season for extra income. And he was a volunteer fireman and ambulance driver. He was never "cooler" in my eyes than when he peeled out of the driveway on his way to the fire station.

And while, out of necessity, he was all work and very little play, he was playful. When I was a little girl I had a disgusting habit. Actually I had many disgusting habits but one stands out. When my hair was long enough, I stuck wads of it in my mouth. Dad told me if I didn't stop my hair would turn to caterpillars. To prove his point he had me spit in a glass of water, then put a hair in the glass overnight. And wouldn't you know it, the next day my hair was gone, replaced by a caterpillar. I haven't chewed my hair since.

During one thunderstorm, he told us that the thunder was the sound of God's pulling his potato wagon in the sky. Sure enough, after the storm passed we were out picking up potatoes in the yard.

And once when I was young girl I tried to make perfume by soaking rose petals in water. But my perfume turned out more stinky than rosy. Mom told me later the odor probably had something to do with the whiskey Dad had added to my perfume. I suppose that would do it.

My father died a few days after I graduated from college. My mother died in 2013 at the age of 96. I am in awe of the sacrifice and wisdom it took for them to raise ten children successfully. We're all still speaking to each other. We've all gone on to lead fairly productive lives. And we all have plenty of bathrooms.

VII
No More Pencils, No More Books, No More Teenager's Dirty Looks

Don't Bite the Hand That Pays for Your Braces

Apparently I make a little clicking sound when I chew. This might not be such a problem if I didn't chew so often. It's not that noticeable, though, so please don't hesitate to invite me to dinner. Honestly my eleven-year-old son is the only one to mention it—but he's mentioned it a lot.

Not only that, but my dainty little mouth is not large enough for my teeth. (I know what you're thinking, but it's true.) Unfortunately I wasn't enlightened enough to know I had crooked teeth until it was brought to my attention by a young man I dated back in college. We had been together for quite some time when he told me he was thinking of buying me a very expensive, somewhat shiny gift. Well what would you think?

As it turns out he meant braces. I'm not kidding. At the time I would never have let him spend that kind of money on me. Now I wish I would have.

Amazingly, my self-esteem remained intact after that relationship. But years later a dentist told me that braces would not only make the clicking sound go away, they would make me feel better about my smile. Wonderful, except that up until that moment I'd felt fine about my smile, despite the efforts of my former boyfriend.

So when Isaac's dentist recommended we see an orthodontist I followed directions. I want him to grow up healthy. And I want to save him from embarrassment. From my perspective getting braces was an act of love and parental responsibility, not to mention extreme self-sacrifice. My son didn't see it that way.

Amazingly there was a time when he thought braces were cool. Naturally that was before he had them. Once he had them, it took him no time to decide they aren't cool at all. He may have made up his mind before he got out of the orthodontist's chair—maybe even before he got into it.

He immediately vowed to stop eating everything except for ice cream and tapioca pudding until the braces come off in two years. Just as well; that might be all I can afford to feed him now. If he follows through he's going to be emaciated. He'll probably stop growing, and as he's quick to point out, it will be my fault. I tell him he shouldn't bite the hand that pays for his braces.

At least he'll have a nice smile. Not that he'll ever flash it at me again. Ironically he doesn't care what his smile is going to look like when the braces are off, or even what it looks like now that they're on. Appearance would have been a big issue for me when I was his age. But one hardly notices braces today. In modern middle schools they're almost as common as teeth.

My son's major concerns are discomfort, difficulty eating and giving up soda pop. We asked a friend of his who had recently had his braces removed for tips on coping with these and the many other inconveniences of braces. He had only one suggestion, but it was a good one: "Try not to say S. You might spit on someone."

I hadn't even thought of that. My main concerns all along have been: one, can a child live on ice cream alone? And two, will I be forced to stand on the street corner with a bucket that says, "Please help. My son just got braces."

But out of concern for my child I have made this great sacrifice. His teeth will be perfect in his graduation photos, assuming we can afford them. His children will never comment on his chewing. And no girlfriend of his is ever going to offer to buy him braces.

Hey, wait a minute.

Worry Works

It's 29 degrees. I'm wearing long johns, wool pants, a turtleneck, an alpaca sweater and a parka. I barely fit behind the wheel. My teenager is wearing a hoodie and jeans. I'll worry about him the rest of the day and it's a darn good thing.

Mother Nature has endowed human moms with the most powerful adaptation there is to protect our young, and that's worry. I'm not joking. Most of what we worry about doesn't happen, so it must work.

My son has survived all sorts of worrisome things. He climbs trees. He goes days without eating a vegetable. He drives, for heaven's sake. The only thing keeping him from catastrophe is the protective benefit of his mother's worry. Not that it's easy. Nothing worthwhile ever is.

As children grow up their mothers grow old and die. That's no coincidence. If I look middle-aged it's because worrying about my child has made me look that way. Also because I am.

But if the aging process in mothers is hastened by fretting about their children, aging in fathers is hastened by listening to mothers fret. So it's best if I keep it to myself while I singlehandedly do the worrying for the whole family. Lucky for them, I'm so good at it.

When my son was three he tasted our dieffenbachia. If you're a worrier like I am, you know those are not safe to eat. I called poison control and gave Isaac milk to drink like they suggested. More importantly I checked his breathing every two hours and worried in between. And it was worth it. Not only did he survive, he didn't even get sick.

Years later, a chinchilla he was pet sitting in our home took a bite out of the same plant. Naturally my son was concerned. I told him not to worry so he didn't. He went to bed, fell asleep faster than you can say "dieffenbachia" and had to be rousted out of bed in the morning. Meanwhile I got up three times in the night to check the chinchilla. It was fine thanks to me.

Yes, my worry is powerful stuff. The downside is it exhausts me and annoys my son. "Drive carefully, honey. There are maniacs out there." "Put lettuce on that sandwich; it's probably the only vegetable you'll eat all week." "Dress warmly. Haven't you ever heard of the polar vortex?"

Then I find his coat on the basement floor and I stew about frostbite and hypothermia all day until he bounds through the door, alive and well, that evening. See, I told you. It works.

Life, Liberty and the Pursuit of a New Ford Mustang

Of all the professions that require patience, driver education teacher must be right up there with daycare provider and hostage negotiator. I delegated the responsibility of teaching Isaac to drive to a professional—driver education teacher, not hostage negotiator—and to my exceptionally patient husband. I hoped this would preserve both my relationship with my son and my own sanity. Besides I'm not that good a driver.

I'm happy to report that so far our relationship remains intact. I can't say the same for my sanity. I know all parents of new drivers understand what I mean. You watch your child slide behind the wheel of a 3,000-pound vehicle and all you can think about is, "I once watched that child wreck a tricycle."

Worse, having them make comments like, "Dad, aren't you following a little close?" or "Mom, did you remember to use your blinker?" can be disconcerting, especially when you didn't.

You're also haunted by the knowledge that soon your child will be asking for the car on a regular basis. You'll find yourself bumming rides from him—in your own vehicle. And you'll only see her briefly when she comes home to sleep or when she walks across the stage at graduation.

But there are benefits to having a new driver in the home. For example you won't have to run to the store in the middle of making dinner anymore, though you might have to delay your preparations while your child takes the long way home. And if you get sleepy on family trips you can always have your newly-licensed teen take over. Believe me, that will keep you awake.

There are a few things you should keep in mind before you pass off the car keys.

Many new drivers want sporty cars, but for safety reasons they should only be allowed to drive larger cars, minivans or armored trucks. These vehicles are not the "chick magnets" or "man mobiles" they're hoping for, but I'm sure I don't have to tell you that's a good thing.

Limit the number of teens that can ride in the car while your child is driving. Studies show that the IQ of a teenage driver is inversely proportional to the number of teenagers he or she is transporting. This doesn't surprise me since my own IQ is also inversely proportional to the number of teenagers I'm transporting.

Teens tend to be in a hurry. Remind your new driver that a great deal of time can be wasted while he visits with a highway patrolman.

Assure your new driver that you definitely want her to finish her homework, comb her hair and eat plenty of nutritious food; you just don't want her doing any of it while she's driving.

And under no circumstances is your child to use his cell phone while he's driving. But be ready with a wise parental response when he says, "But you do." In case you're wondering the wise parental response might be something like, "If I jumped off a cliff would you do that too?" or maybe "At least I don't text when I drive." Then he'll say, "You couldn't text and drive at the same time even if I held the wheel for you." I don't have a wise parental response for that.

Finally remind your teen that life, liberty and the pursuit of happiness are rights. Driving is not a right; it's a privilege. Privileges must be earned and can be lost. Then be prepared with another wise parental response when your child says, "It would be easier to pursue my happiness in a new Ford Mustang."

You're All Minnows Now

I suspect there are two things people who are about to graduate get tired of: being asked what they're going to do next and being told what they ought to do next.

We're not asking because we're nosey—well, some of us are nosey. It's just that graduation makes us look back wistfully at that time in our own lives. The world is an oyster for new graduates but we feel like old crabs.

And as for giving advice, we care about our graduates enough to want to save them from learning life lessons the way we did—the hard way. Still, we know they won't listen. And the reason we know it is because when we were their age, we didn't listen either. So here's the advice I'd give graduates if they'd read this book, which I'm quite sure they will not.

1. I'd tell them that this is a new day. Good or bad, whatever they were in the phase of life they're graduating from, they start with a clean slate in the next one. It won't matter anymore whether they were little guppies in a big lake or big fish in a mud puddle; they're all minnows now. (I'm not sure why seafood plays so prominently in metaphors about the future but it may have something to do with all the fish sticks they ate as children.)

2. I'd tell them that graduation shouldn't signal the end of learning. The educational system "on the outside" is different—no grades, no finals, no summers off. But there are teachers and learning opportunities everywhere. Life-long learners are more interesting and sometimes even better paid. Plus we never know when we might wind up on *Jeopardy* or *Who Wants To Be A Millionaire?*

3. I would tell them to be kind to everyone they meet; we never know who might win the lottery next. I'm joking! I wouldn't tell them that, but I would tell them to be kind to everyone they meet. Mean people have more enemies and more digestive disorders, and if they don't, they should.

4. I'd tell graduates that it behooves us all to use our talents fully and only for good. If any graduate I know uses writing talent to become a tabloid journalist or technology skills to become an identity thief, I'm taking my graduation gift back.

5. I'd tell them that adversity makes us smarter, wiser, stronger and kinder, or it makes us grumpy and mean. We all choose. And while I sincerely hope the graduates I know don't face much adversity, if they do I hope they don't choose grumpy and mean.

6. I'd tell them they're never too young to take care of their health. Graduates don't realize this now but they're mere mortals, just like the rest of us. Young people can be cavalier about their health. I know plenty of middle-aged people who were too, right up until their first heart attack. They became a lot more health-conscious after that.

7. I would tell them that before they envy what others have, they should consider the possibility that those with many material possessions may have a lot of money or they may have a lot of debt. We should assume the latter if it makes us feel better.

8. I would tell graduates that wherever they roam from now on, they should keep in mind that someone somewhere is worrying about them. Most likely it's their mothers. They should visit their parents often and call between visits. And

I'd say, "Call, don't just text." They'd grumble, but it's not like I'd tell them to write letters.

Job Hunting with Sweet Cheeks

Back when I started in the job market embarrassing information about job seekers had a way of getting around town. Today it has a way of getting around the globe which, as you know, is somewhat bigger. Parents of job seekers can't help but worry—especially if they've seen their child's Facebook page.

If you're a parent who's finding it hard to discuss your concerns, insert the following into your son or daughter's graduation card. (Hint: your child will be more likely to read it if you don't put any cash in the card.)

Congratulations! We're so proud of you. We wish you an exciting future and a fulfilling career that pays so well that you never have to move back in with us. (Don't take that wrong. You wouldn't like it any more than we would.)

We know how much you hate unsolicited advice. But since you never solicit any you leave us no choice.

We realize your generation is smarter about technology than those most likely to be doing the hiring. But after years of having children program their VCRs, managers aren't the least bit embarrassed to ask their fifth grade neighbors to help them locate information about job applicants on the Internet. And while stories about underage drinking and letting pigs loose during graduation might make you popular with your friends, your friends probably aren't in a position to hire you right now.

Also please avoid mentioning how much you despised your last employer on your blog unless you're independently wealthy and will never need to work again—which would be news to us.

Online applications were not around when we were starting out, mainly because computers hadn't been invented yet. But there are some rules that still apply. Never answer the question, "reason for leaving your last job," with "I hated getting up early."

As far as accomplishments go, the fact that you can juggle, drink milk through your nose and text faster than your mother can type may not be relevant. And as deserving as you were of the honor years ago, neither is being voted Most Beautiful Baby in 1995.

There are some issues that those of us who applied for jobs on paper (or stone) did not have to consider. For example, before you start filling out applications consider updating your email address. You may not convey the professional image employers are looking for with a handle like "couchsurfer" or "sweetcheeks@something.com."

As you know, some modern parents have been accused of being over-involved in their children's lives. That doesn't describe us. Still, no matter how much we beg, *do not* let us go to a job interview with you.

And we don't mean to nag but please dress appropriately for job interviews. Different work places have different standards, but in general you should avoid flip-flops, sweatpants and underwear that shows. Likewise your midriff should never show during a job interview, in part because a middle-aged interviewer will be jealous that yours is still worth showing.

Yes, we know you're old enough to get a tattoo without permission but we'd suggest you hold off on any large tattoos in obvious places until you're employed (and maybe even after), unless you're working in a tattoo parlor and you're sure you'll want to be there until you retire, which is a long way off.

Remember to turn off your cell phone. A job interview is no time to take a call and texting would be very distracting to both you and the interviewer.

Now go get 'em! Your whole wonderful life lies ahead. Don't forget us when you get to the top! And don't forget your college loans either.

An Empty Nest Full of Sour Milk

For a lot of parents the reality of the empty nest hits them like a crate of high school yearbooks that day they walk into their child's vacant bedroom. Not me. When my son flew the coop more than a year ago he left a whole lot of stuff behind in the nest. Even now when I walk into his bedroom, I can hardly tell he's gone.

So no, it wasn't the room that brought empty nest home for me. It hit me that day I tasted sour milk for the first time in 18 years. Milk was never around long enough to go bad when Isaac was home. There were times when he was growing up I'd considered buying a milk cow.

Now all of sudden the milk has soured and so have a few other things. For one, my sincere belief that for all these years he was the one leaving lights on in empty rooms and dirty dishes all over the house. And he was the one eating the Easter candy long before Easter and the Halloween candy before the trick-or-treaters arrived. Now I know better. So do our trick-or-treaters.

Then he came home for a visit and I had another shock. Apparently, all the while I was raising my son to think for himself I was assuming it would be exactly like I think, because, well, I'm right. Now I often find myself fervently praying the prayer of the empty nest mom: Dear Lord, guide my child when we're apart and my mouth when we're together.

Yes, it's not easy watching your chicks leave the nest but don't let me scare you. You've been in training for this. If your children are like Isaac was you'll hardly see them during their senior year anyway. I'd notice food missing from the fridge. I'd hear the shower in the basement now and then. I'd see his belongings scattered around but other than that, there was little evidence he lived here at all. It was like having a travel writer rent our basement—a travel writer who never paid his rent.

But my son was preparing me and I appreciate it in the way you appreciate a flu shot. It hurts for a while but it keeps you from getting really sick later on.

I look at it this way: We spend all those years raising them to be independent, and darn it, it works. I'm guessing the only thing harder than having your children leave the nest is having them decide they never will.

Made in the USA
Monee, IL
03 November 2020